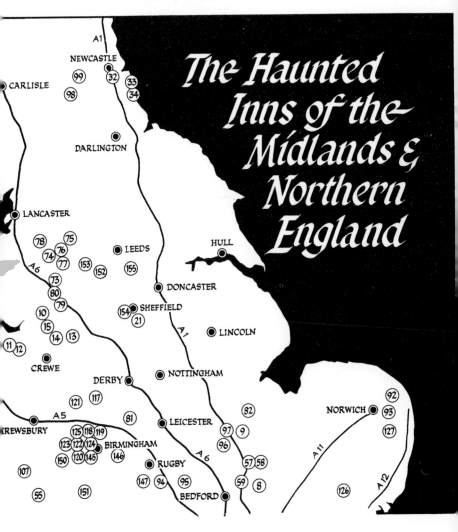

The Haunted Inns of the Midlands & Northern England

TO JUNE

for everything

by Jack Hallam

Photographs by *Chris Thornton*

Wolfe Publishing Limited
10 Earlham Street, London WC2

Every effort was made, at the time of going to press, to check telephone numbers, opening hours, details of food and accommodation, etc. It is possible, however, that some of these details may since have changed.

SBN 7234 0474 7

Printed in Great Britain by
Morrison and Gibb Ltd, London & Edinburgh

Contents

Illustrations

Photographs by Chris Thornton on pages: 28, 64, 69, 80/81, 94, 95, 96, 102, 104, 112/113, 127, 130, 135, 144, 145, 156/157, 190, 194, 196, 202, 213, 215, 217.

Introduction

by James Wentworth Day

(Author of **In Search of Ghosts, The Ghost-Hunter's Game-Book** and **Here Are Ghosts and Witches.**)

NO HOUSE should be more haunted than an ancient inn. The inn is almost the perfect microcosm of humanity. To it come the traveller on his way, the lonely in search of company, the friendly and the ribald to join in merriment, the gloomy to forget their gloom, the poor in search of warmth, the old to recapture memories, the young to meet their friends and sometimes those tired of life to end their life.

Add the highwayman of old, the footpad of past centuries and the thugs and burglars of today with ears wide open to pick up local knowledge of people and places worth robbing and you have pretty well a complete cross-section of the good and bad in mankind. Rich ground to breed ghosts.

If one was to take a minute survey of the haunted houses in England, it is more than likely that the old inns would beat the moated granges by a short head if not by a few lengths.

So it was high time that someone with an eye for a wraith, an ear for a silken rustle and a nose for clotted blood sought out the ghosts which enrich our ancient hostelries. Jack Hallam has done a job which needed doing. He has collected a rare, rich gallimaufry of ghosts. I know some of his inns and I know that what he writes about them is true.

It is idle to deny the existence of ghosts. Too many level-headed people who do not normally seek publicity admit to having seen them. After all, is there any reason *why* they should not exist? A hundred years ago our grandparents would have been accused of witchcraft if they had been able to press a switch and turn on the light. To pick up a telephone and talk to someone on the other side of the world. To press another switch and throw on a screen life-size figures of men and women in full colour walking and talking in every country on earth. It was unheard of and unthinkable that man should be able to transmit voices and portraits of people without visible means to any corner of the world. It was even more unthinkable that man should fly to the moon.

Is it therefore unthinkable that at times, usually at very odd times, the ghosts of those who are dead should return to the places they knew? I believe, after many years of study of the subject, that some people undoubtedly possess an extra-sensory perception which enables them, usually without premeditation, to see ghosts. Animals, particularly dogs and horses, have a sixth sense which we do not begin to understand. That sixth sense lingers in some human beings.

A ghostly visitation is, in a sense, a reappearance of past people or events thrown for an instant on what we may perhaps describe as the cinema-screen of time. Those events may have been tragic, violent, sentimental, founded on deep hates or enduring passions. Sometimes, as in the case of the well-known ghost which appeared to various people in the Earl of Powis' house in Berkeley Square, the ghost returns to its former home in order to remedy an old wrong. In that particular instance, the ghost returned to rediscover a hidden box containing important family papers. Once the box of papers was discovered the ghost never appeared again. Its job was done.

In the case of one inn which I know, The Bear at Stock in Essex, about which Mr Hallam writes, it is a fact that the ghost or ghosts 'vet' each new tenant of the inn. If they do not approve of him the tenant has a very uncomfortable time. If the ghosts decide that the tenant is the right man for such a splendid old house they trouble him no further.

Mr Hallam has gone the length and breadth of England to find his ghosts, his facts and his stories on the spot. He has done a great work and added an invaluable chapter to the age-old history of this country.

It is a book to buy and keep—a book to take in the car when you drive out into the country or put in your pocket when you walk the field paths to the inn beyond the hill.

Bedfordshire

Lovely Lady Gray

1 **THE GEORGE, Silsoe.**
A Greene King house in the High Street. Open : 10 to 2.30 & 6 to 10.30. Sunday : 12 to 2.30 & 7 to 10.30. Lunches and dinner. Accommodation. Parking. Nearest station : Flitwick. Telephone : Silsoe 218.

THE GREY LADY of The George was a headstrong beauty of wealth. She is the ghost of Lady Elizabeth Gray, daughter of a well-to-do local family, who fell in love with a coachman from the inn and hid there for two weeks until their plan to elope was discovered by her angry father. In making their getaway their coach ran off the road into a lake and Lady Elizabeth was drowned. In 1959 the landlady, tired of having the girl's ghost about the place—opening doors and causing disturbances in the night—advertised in a pub trade paper for 'a layer for the Silsoe ghost' . . . Members of the Birmingham Psychic Society offered their services at the 240-year-old inn and spent a weekend making an inconclusive search.

Berkshire

The Phantom Lodger

2   WHITE HART, Moneyrow Green, Holyport.
A Morland house, two miles south of the M4 on B3024. Open:
10.30 to 2.30 & 6 to 10.30. Sunday: 12 to 2 & 7 to 10.30. Parking.
Nearest station: Maidenhead. Telephone: Maidenhead 20080.

AIR RAID SIRENS had howled into the night sky and German bombers were blitzing London when Mrs Gladys Bennett had her first confrontation with the ghost at the White Hart. She was more unnerved by the sound of bombing in the distance than by the ghost of a young woman in a grey cloak, who cradled a baby in her arms.

'We were all sleeping downstairs at the time,' says Mrs Bennett. 'My husband was asleep on a separate camp bed and it looked as if this woman was sitting on my husband's head with the young baby in her arms. As I reached out to touch her she disappeared.'

Since that night nearly 30 years ago Mrs Bennett has seen the Grey Lady several times. So did the previous licensee. Before the ghost materialises there is always the sound of footsteps coming down the stairs, which sends the dogs into a frenzy. There is also loud banging from behind the panelling. This banging has been heard by several other people but only Mrs Bennett has seen the ghost; it usually appears in the private sitting-room at the rear of the house.

Until a few years ago Mrs Bennett used to wait up at night as Christmas approached, because then it was that her phantom lodger, as the Grey Lady has been nicknamed, invariably appeared.

Like a number of others of the same name, this White Hart Inn was once within the Royal Forest of Windsor. What was once a game-keeper's cottage was promoted over the years to a hunting lodge used by many a monarch, for picnicking between kills.

*   *   *

The White Hart has another visitant—a phantom horse. It is heard—and occasionally seen—galloping up to the pub and then away again. Some local folk suggest it is the ghost of the steeple-chaser Kruger. In the year 1901 Kruger fell at an open ditch at nearby Hawthorn Hill race course. The horse rolled on his rider, who was killed.

Mine Host the Ghost

3   THE NEW INN, Blewbury.
This is a free house recently renamed The Blueberry Inn. It is on A417 Goring to Harwell road. Open : 10 to 2.30 & 6 to 10.30. Sunday : 12 to 2 & 7 to 10.30. Food at bar. Parking. Nearest station : Didcot (4 mls.). Telephone : Blewbury 496.

'OLD EDWIN' as regulars call him, walks from an upstairs bedroom, which used to be his, to the bar downstairs. His footsteps are described as 'hollow and rubbery', the sound made as if by somebody walking in wellington boots. The ghostly footsteps are thought to be those of Edwin Fry, who was landlord at the pub until his death in 1951.

Mystery of the Teardrop Room

4   THE GEORGE HOTEL, Wallingford.
A free house in the town centre. Open : 10 to 2.30 & 6 to 10.30. Friday and Saturday to 11. Sunday : 12 to 2 & 7 to 10.30. Snacks, lunches and dinner. Accommodation : 16 bedrooms. Parking. Nearest station : Didcot. Telephone : Wallingford 2587.

ROOM NO. 3 of The George is no ordinary hotel room, not because it is supposed to be haunted, but because this is the Teardrop Room, in which the walls are painstakingly plastered in an intricate teardrop pattern. That, in an inn with a 12th-century pedigree makes it uniquely historic.

It is said, though most improbably, that the ghost which haunts this room was a mistress of King Charles I who shut herself up and cried herself to death when told of his execution. Variations on that theme are many, all stemming from the story that the King was lodged at a house opposite The George while en route to London and the scaffold.

The Sign of the George Hotel, Wallingford (No. 4)

There is also the legend that the girl who imprisoned herself in Room No. 3 and died broken-hearted, to return as a ghost, was the daughter of a man who disapproved of her lover and killed him in a brawl. They probably fought in the yard where Sam Pearse, the landlord in 1636, had a brew house in which he concocted his own brew of Wallingford ale.

A hundred years on and Turpin was abroad on the roads. He is thought to have put up at The George, occupying the room overlooking the archway leading to the inn yard, to ensure himself of a chance of escape via the window.

But surely Turpin is too busy putting in nightly appearances elsewhere to be able to include The George on his ghostly rounds.

There is, however, another haunting. In Room No. 5 the figures of two small children have been seen standing by the wash basin. To the guest who saw this apparition, it was so vivid and the figures looked so solid that she woke her husband to confirm what she had seen. Since that night three years ago other guests have said—independently and without prior knowledge of the ghost children—that they had the feeling of not being alone when in the room.

Buckinghamshire

The Screaming Phantom

5   THE CHEQUERS, Old Amersham.
*A Benskin Ind Coope house in old Amersham. Open : 10 to 2.30 &
6 to 10.30. Sunday : 12 to 2 & 7 to 10.30. Nearest station : Amersham.
Telephone : Amersham 5736.*

THE MARTYRS of Buckinghamshire are many. Some, like Thomas
Chase, were killed in prison. Others, such as William Tylsworth, were
burned. Many were manacled, fettered and loaded with irons and left
to die. Those from Amersham who suffered for their faith are remembered by a memorial in a field just off the Chesham road, and more
dramatically by the haunting of The Chequers. Some of those who went
to the stake spent their last hours in this building and that is said to
account for the 'weird shrieking screams echoing through the building
at night'.
   The quote is from a former landlord who moved because he and his
wife were kept awake by the sounds and his two small daughters talked
of seeing a hooded figure in their bedroom. It has been suggested that
the pub is not haunted by the ghost of one of the martyrs, but by the
tormented spirit of the only daughter of William Tylsworth. She was
made to light the fire which consumed her father.

His Violin Tucked Underneath His Arm...

6   WHITE HART, Chalfont St Peter.
*A Benskin house on the Amersham to Gerrards Cross road (A413).
Open : 10 to 2.30 & 6 to 10.30. (Friday and Saturday to 11.) Sunday :
12 to 2 & 7 to 10.30. Food served. Public car park opposite. Nearest
station : Gerrards Cross. Telephone : Chalfont St Giles 2441.*

TAKE NO NOTICE of the sound of footsteps in the 14th-century attic.
You can hear the like in a dozen other pubs—but not the violin playing.
That's free by courtesy of the White Hart management of 50 years ago.

23

The landlord then was Donald Ross who played his fiddle in the bar by way of entertainment right up to the year he died at the age of 70.

Some years ago when an old friend stayed overnight, the landlord woke next morning at the sound of someone going down the creaking stairs—as he thought—to put the kettle on. He lay back in anticipation of his friend bringing him a cup of tea in bed. Two rooms away the friend was having a lie-in too, since he thought he'd heard the landlord go down to the kitchen. And so he had—the ghostly landlord with his violin under his arm.

The Tragic Serving Wench

7   GEORGE AND DRAGON, West Wycombe.
A Courage hotel on the A40 main High Wycombe to Oxford road. Open : 10 to 2.30 & 6 to 10.30. Sunday : 12 to 2 & 7 to 10.30. Accommodation : 10 doubles. Lunch and dinner. Ample parking. Nearest station : High Wycombe. Telephone : High Wycombe 23602.

SUKIE WAS MORE than just a pretty face. She had a pretty figure too that did its best to escape from the revealing tightness of her laced bodice—and at times almost succeeded. She loathed the long voluminous dresses she had to wear as a serving-maid at the George and Dragon, since they covered her shapely legs and left showing only her large, bare feet.

She was an ambitious 16-year-old, an outrageous flirt with an insatiable appetite for men, and she made sure that she got her share of the opportunities with every coach-load of travellers that swung into the inn yard. Sometimes it was a coach making for Oxford, some twenty-odd miles away, swarming with young men, gay, flattering, devil-take-the-hindmost. Or else a coach heading for London, full of merchants, moneyed, prosperous and indulgent.

The George and Dragon was a regular stopping-place for the 18th-century traveller passing along the narrow cottage-lined West Wycombe High Street. It was well known for its bed and board—as it is today—and equally as well known for its close proximity to the nefarious Hell-Fire Club, a league of debauched notables and their womenfolk who indulged in orgies in the caves that Sir Francis Dashwood had had cut deep into the chalk hillside overlooking the village.

From the musty little attic bedroom Sukie shared with two other serving girls, she could hear the chatter and hilarity of the gentlemen and their 'ladies' as they made their way back from the caves to the big house in West Wycombe Park. She made up her mind that was for her—a life of love and luxury—by way of the richest and handsomest customer who would have her. To this end Sukie worked hard, imitating the airs and graces of the gentlewomen who stayed at the inn, and in particular learning about the things that pleased and satisfied the men she fancied.

There were few among the locals rich enough to give her the good life she aspired to. But among those who stayed overnight at the George and Dragon, there were plenty, both elegant and dashing enough to turn Sukie's pretty head. For them she'd do anything—and did . . . until that wet, blustery night the good-looking stranger clattered over the cobbles of the inn yard and dismounted from his exhausted chestnut mare.

Sukie served him with wine at one of the copper-topped tables in the noisy dining-room, and eyed him from a distance through the haze of tobacco smoke as he waited for his food. Deliberately she took a little longer in carrying it to his table so that she could get a long look at him.

He certainly looked prosperous as well as ruggedly handsome. He wore good clothes and carried a purseful of sovereigns so by the time Sukie put the heaped plate of game pie in front of him she had made up her mind he was nothing less than a nobleman and, to her way of thinking, a very attractive one at that.

He didn't stay the night, only half the night, lingering with Sukie in the hayloft above the stall in which his mare pawed the flagstones restlessly. Dawn was only an hour or two away when he cantered noisily out of the sleeping village.

Eyes Only For Sukie

But the next night he was back, seated alone at the same table. He introduced himself to no one, talked only small talk with the casual travellers who addressed themselves to him. It was plain to anybody who cared enough to notice that it was only Sukie he had come to see. He would sit, supping his ale, watching Sukie as she waited on those who came and went. Often it was past midnight before the last of the travellers had gone to bed and Sukie had finished her kitchen chores. Then he was able to meet her in the inn yard.

There were nights during the next few weeks when he didn't come. Sometimes two or three nights in a row. Then Sukie's other admirers, jealous of her new-found lover, would jibe at her mockingly, calling her 'Your Ladyship.' The coarser among them took even bigger liberties, which was easy enough in the crowded, dimly-lit public room.

And that's where they thought up their plan to get even with this cheeky serving wench who had ambitions that didn't become her.

The ostler's boy was an easy victim of their scheming. For the price of a pot of ale he agreed to give Sukie a message, supposedly from her lover, passed to him, he said, by the driver of the last stage from Oxford.

It was a simple message; to be in the chalk caves at midnight, dressed in a gown of white.

To Sukie that meant one thing only. Half an hour before midnight she was there waiting, her voluminous white gown, borrowed from the cook's sister, flapping round her trim ankles. As the time dragged by she began to get uneasy as well as cold. When she had just about forced herself to accept that it was a trick and that she should go back to the George and Dragon before it was too late, she heard voices, loud mocking voices. Her spurned admirers, wild with too much strong ale, rushed at her out of the darkness. While one held aloft a flaming torch, the others grabbed at the petrified girl and ripped her 'wedding dress' from her shoulders. Kicking and clawing was her only defence against their drunken strength.

But in a second it was all over for Sukie. Overwhelmed by the sudden-ness of the attack, she lost her balance, staggered backwards and struck her head on the wall of the cave as she fell to the floor.

In the morning Sukie was found dead in her bedroom, carried there by three frightened men, whose plan to teach her a lesson had gone tragically wrong.

The same three men and the ostler's boy carried her to her grave, wrapped in her makeshift wedding dress, and there are those who like to believe that Sukie's handsome lover—a nobleman perhaps, though more likely a successful highwayman—watched her burial from the shelter of the trees, sitting astride his chestnut steed.

The White Lady

A few days after Sukie's death, such strange things began to happen in the room she had shared with the other serving maids that the two girls moved out. One wonders if they, all of 200 years ago, experienced happenings similar to those described by Mr Jhan Robbins, an Ameri-can from Connecticut, who stayed there in 1966 and wrote this about it in *Reader's Digest*:

'I saw a pinpoint of light glowing about three feet off the ground near the door . . . I watched the shaft of light grow wider and stronger. It had an opaque pearly quality. The apparition of the White Lady—if indeed it was she—was now about two feet in diameter and four feet high, still hovering near the doorway . . . I flung back the covers and carrying my heavy book in one hand walked resolutely towards the door . . . A few feet from the door I abruptly entered a zone of intense cold. My breathing became laboured. My arms and legs felt heavy . . . As I stood there I was swept by sudden anguished depression, Weltsch-merz, world sadness. Life seemed futile, beset by tragedy. Life must have felt like this to poor Sukie, I thought, with no one to stand up and protect her dignity.

'At this sympathetic feeling, the light ballooned forward and seemed to reach for me. I backed hastily across the room, jumped into bed and yanked the electric light on.'

*   *   *

The night I stopped at the George and Dragon, in that very same room, I slept like a top. So did my friend Charlie Goldblatt. It was a wild night of wind and rain that charged at the window panes as if deter-mined to smash a way into the room and tear us from our beds. Hope-fully we sat up till long past midnight, the tape recorder recording the sound of the elements and the traffic splashing along the road outside.

But no Sukie came to look for her lover, though hers is not the only ghost to haunt this hotel. Footsteps—thought to be those of a traveller whose body was sealed up in the room in which he was murdered in the late 18th century—have been heard night after night, walking very distinctly down the main stairway.

When the BBC sent a television camera team to record the re-opening of the sealed room, a few years ago, they had no better luck than I did in my quest for the White Lady. All that was revealed to them was the dust of two centuries.

The Caxton Gibbet, Caxton (No. 8)

28

Cambridgeshire

Murder in the Shade of the Gibbet

8   THE CAXTON GIBBET, Caxton.
A Paine (of St Neots) house, on A45, nine miles west of Cambridge, at the junction with A14. Open: 10 to 2.30 & 6 to 10.30. Sunday: 12 to 2 & 7 to 10.30. Snacks and lunches. Accommodation. Parking. Nearest station: St Neots. Telephone: Caxton 250.

ONCE HEREABOUTS stood the gibbet from which a host of criminals —highwaymen and less romantic ruffians or unfortunates—were hanged.

This was an obvious place for an inn, since here in 1633 one of the first three toll gates was set up to raise money for the upkeep of the roads.

The landlord of that first inn which grew up alongside the tollhouse was a scoundrel, not above any villainy, even cold-blooded killing if he could profit by it.

Wealthy travellers often lodged at the inn and went on their way next morning, many of them unaware that they had been relieved of their valuables: it was not difficult for the publican to ensure that they slept well. When three blatantly prosperous looking gentlemen arrived one night and asked to be put up the innkeeper could hardly wait for them to stagger off to bed before laying hands on their fat purses.

While he was in their room rifling their belongings, one of the three, not properly asleep, sat up in bed to see what had disturbed him. The landlord smashed his iron fist into the man's face. He murdered all three. He tore the rings from their fingers then dumped their bodies in the well from where the inn drew its water supply.

That act of violence left behind a haunting, which caused travellers who stopped regularly at the old Caxton Gibbet, before it was modernised and extended in 1930, to ask the landlord not to put them in Room No. 5. There the murders were committed—a room which never gets warm, despite a very efficient central heating system.

Successive landlords have lived with the ghost. Its visitations take the form of loud, clear footsteps in the night, stomping from the door of No. 5 along the balcony and down the stairs. At the foot of these stairs, below a trap door, is the well.

'I have heard these footsteps on many occasions,' says one former landlord of the Caxton Gibbet. 'They never returned up the stairs Occasionally I peeped out of my bedroom to see who it was—but there has never been anybody or anything to see. . . .'

It is reasonable to suppose that the murdering innkeeper of long ago ended his days on the gibbet arm outside his own pub. Then, as happened to all the thieves and cut-throats hanged at Caxton, after his bones had been picked bare by the crows, he would have been cut down and buried at Croxton, three miles west on the road to St Neots.

*   *   *

A pub called The Spread Eagle stands on the edge of a long forgotten rogues' cemetery which is thought to be haunted by ghosts of those who died on the gibbet.

Past landlords have reported noises in the night—long after closing time—as if the bars were filled with people making all kinds of noises

'When we first moved in we couldn't sleep for these sounds,' commented Mr Arthur Howe, a former landlord: 'I often got up and had a look around the place to see if I could find the cause. I never did.'

Return of the Lodger

9   **THE BLACK BULL, Whittlesey.**
A Watney house in Market Street. Open: 10 to 2.30 & 6 to 10.30. Sunday: 12 to 2 & 7 to 10.30. Snacks. Accommodation. Nearest station: Whittlesey. Telephone: Whittlesey 3323.

LEGEND SAYS that some time in the 14th century the monks who built the local church used the Black Bull as a lodging-house Since those distant days one of their number has returned from time to time as a ghost haunting the sealed attic and the winding uneven staircase leading to it. 'Charlie Presence' as regulars at the Black Bull call it, was last active in 1963 when the inn was undergoing extensive structural alterations.

The Child in the Mirror

0 YE OLDE NO. 3, Bollington, near Altrincham.
A John Smith House, midway between Lymm and Altrincham on the A56 road. Open: 11.30 to 3 & 5.30 to 10.30. Sunday: 12 to 2 & 7 to 10. Nearest station: Warrington Bank Quay. Telephone: Lymm 2704.

IT'S AN ODD name for a pub. Was it that the landlord couldn't abide the thought of another Pig and Whistle or Spotted Cow? Or was it the brewers who ran out of names and gave it a number instead? It was very nearly like that. This was an inn on the coach road from Liverpool to York; in fact, it was the third call out of Liverpool so it was very simply christened 'No. 3' by the stage drivers who made it the last stop on their return.

In the village of Bollington there are people who will tell you that Ye Olde No. 3 is haunted by the ghost of a gipsy woman, who, on the run from the law, tripped and fell exhausted into a flooded stream. But I prefer this more recent story of the haunting of this pub with such a unique name. It is reprinted from the brewer's house magazine:

'When the light fades and evening falls, the low ceilings seem lower somehow. Dark corners appear where you never noticed a corner before and the firelight dancing in the grate plays tricks with your eyes. And when you are as warm as toast, pulled well up to a roasting fire and with the interior flow of alcohol, an ice-cold breeze may sweep through the room. A strange chill almost sets your teeth a-chattering. But the doors and windows will be closed tight with nowhere for such a draught to come from. There was an occasion when lights were mysteriously switched on and off and carpets and clothes disarranged. At other times brassware at the pub has been polished during the night.

'It was only a few months ago when the most startling thing of all occurred. Mrs Atherton, the landlord's wife, was in her bedroom alone at three o'clock one morning when she saw a child looking at herself in her dressing-table mirror. "I saw her as clear as a bell," Mrs Atherton recalled. "She wore a blue frock and an old-fashioned poke bonnet and then went through the bedroom door without opening it." '

Hoariest of Them All?

11 GEORGE & DRAGON, Chester.

A Whitbread/Threlfalls house, No. 1 Liverpool Road, in the city centre. Open: 11 to 3 & 5.30 to 10.30. Sunday: 12 to 2 & 7 to 10.30. Snacks at bar. Ample parking. Nearest station: Chester City. Telephone: Chester 22068.

THIS INN, built only 30 years ago, probably has the oldest ghost of them all. It is on the site of a Roman cemetery, no more than 500 yards from the wall of Deva, the fortress city founded by the Romans in the 1st century A.D. The footsteps one hears could be those of a legionnaire on sentry duty. They stomp, loud and clear with measured tread from one end of the upper floor to the other. Twenty minutes later they stomp back again in the opposite direction—and always in the small hours.

Says the landlord, with a hint of one-up-manship, 'If the Romans left Chester in 406 A.D. my ghost should be 1,564 years old at least!' What makes it more credible to suppose that the Roman *does* haunt the George & Dragon is that the upper floor of the pub is divided into 14 rooms by a maze of walls and passages. Only a ghost could walk from one end to the other.

The Headless Housekeeper

12 THE HEADLESS WOMAN, Duddon, near Tarporley.

A Greenall Whitley house, on the Tarporley road, eight miles out of Chester. Open: 11 to 3 & 5.30 to 10.30. Sunday: 12 to 2 & 7 to 10.30. Snacks. Parking. Nearest station: Chester (7 miles). Telephone: Huxley 082/924/252.

THIS PUB is named after the ghost that haunts it, though one wonders which came first—the ghost or the pub? Maybe it was not an inn at all in the first place, but an oil shop, displaying the oilman's sign of the heedless virgins of the Biblical parable. It is even possible that the original inn was named The Good Woman, or The Silent Woman, or perhaps The Quiet Woman. All displayed signs of a woman carrying her head under her arm.

The oil man, a thrifty fellow, kept the same sign above his door when he found it was worth his while to sell beer as well. After that it was only a matter of time before slovenly speech corrupted the heedless virgins into the headless woman.

Until a few years ago there was a wooden figure of a woman outside the pub at Duddon—headless and, in the opinion of some, gruesome like the events that brought about this haunting.

Cromwell with his model army was as ruthless in these parts as in most other places in England. After he had routed Charles's last army at Chester, his soldiers scoured the Cheshire countryside for Royalists

In their search of Duddon Heath they came upon Hockenhull Hall, deserted and stripped of all its valuables. After burying the silver, the family had fled leaving only a handful of servants in the care of the housekeeper. Incensed at finding nothing of any worth and unable to make the jibbering servants tell them where the silver was hidden, the soldiers tortured the housekeeper into insensibility and, as a final act of savagery, hacked her head from her shoulders.

There is a plaque in the inn recording that on many occasions the ghost of this murdered housekeeper has been seen 'carrying her head under her arm, walking along an old bridle path between Hockenhull Hall and the spot where it comes out on the Tarporley road near the public house.'

Over the years several landlords and customers have laid claim to seeing the ghost dressed in her white gown. Most of the sightings have been in or near the inn.

Promiscuous Mary

13 HARRINGTON ARMS, Gawsworth, Macclesfield.
A Robinson (of Stockport) house, on A534. Open : 11.30 to 3 & 5.30 to 10.30. Sandwiches at the bar. Parking. Nearest station : Maccles-field. Telephone : North Rode 325.

MARY FITTON caused quite a stir the day she joined the court of Queen Elizabeth I. She was just 17 and shapely with it, despite the hoop and ruff, which was the unflattering fashion of her day. She was not only good to look at, but she had charm as well as wit, which didn't go unnoticed.

Sir William Knollys, the fifty-year-old Comptroller of the Queen's Household, had her in his charge and fell passionately in love with her. So did William Herbert, friend of Shakespeare and later Earl of Pembroke. He gave her a baby and landed himself in the Fleet prison in consequence. Which may have temporarily curbed his activities, but not Mary's. Though she was sacked by the Queen, she lost no time in having an affair with an old friend of the Fitton family, Sir Richard Leveson, and, according to some, bore him two daughters. A year or so later she had a son by a Captain William Polewhele and then married him, much to the disapproval of her family; they presumably didn't think him good enough.

What they thought of Will Shakespeare, the other man in her life, we will never know. Nobody seems to have put it on record. It is still a big question mark as to whether or not she was ever the bard's mistress. Was the fair-skinned, grey-eyed, promiscuous Mary the Dark Lady of Shakespeare's Sonnets? Or was it her elder, contentedly-married sister Anne, he was swooning over when he wrote:

My mistress' eyes are nothing like the sun,
Coral is more red than her lips are red:
If snow be white why then her breasts are dun;
If hairs be wires, black wires grow on her head;
I have seen roses damask'd red and white,
But no such roses see I in her cheeks.

The answers are as uncertain as her ghost, said to walk in the evening through the long avenue of lime trees, from the Old Hall to the door of the Harrington Arms. It is a walk she must have done often as a girl before she left Gawsworth to join the Queen's court in London, though at that time the Harrington Arms did not exist.

This creeper-covered pub on a bend in the road from Macclesfield to Congleton, is not so old. It was once nothing more than a farmhouse (perhaps doing double duty as a gamekeeper's lodge at the far end of the drive), before becoming a pub, which originally had the delightful name The Load of Hay.

In his book *The Manor of Gawsworth*, Raymond Richards writes: 'It is a rare Queen Anne house, very little changed since it was built. The forecourt is cobbled and the old bar, with its original furniture, is a splendid survival of the early 18th century. It is very much a farmer's and countryman's inn . . . and long may it remain so.'

The Brown Lady

14   OLDE RED LION, Holmes Chapel.
An Ind Coope house on the A50 road at its junction with A54, half a mile east of the M6 motorway. Open: 11 to 3 & 5.30 to 10.30. Sunday 12 to 2 & 7 to 10.30. Meals served. Accommodation: bed and breakfast. Parking. Nearest station: Holmes Chapel. Telephone: Holmes Chapel 2296.

A MINISTRY OF HOUSING report a few years back says this pub 'appears to be of 17th-century origin.' You will not think so as you look at the roughcast stucco exterior. It is a great pity the original ox-blood red bricks were not left exposed, as are the bevelled beams inside. Take note too of the staircase—a splendid piece of craftsmanship— as you go up to what was the sealed-off room, the haunt of the Brown Lady. While upstairs have a look at the prayer dedicated to Prince Charlie, inscribed on a bedroom windowpane, said to be the work of John Wesley who passed that way in the 1750's.

Mary Fitton (right) and her sister Anne

(A Sunday Times *photograph by courtesy of Captain Fitzroy Newdegate)*

'Goodnight Mr Higgins!'

15 ROYAL GEORGE, Knutsford.

A Watney Mann hotel (24 bedrooms). In the town centre on the A50, a short walk from the station. The M6 motorway is about 1½ miles away. Car parks adjoining the hotel and opposite. Open: 11 to 3 & 5.30 to 10.30. Sunday: 12 to 2 & 7 to 10.30. Nearest station: Knutsford. Telephone: Knutsford 4151.

NO BOOK about the haunted inns of England could ignore the Royal George, though it is not any longer an inn, but very much a hotel. When it was the White Swan back in Plantagenet days it earned no mention in the Knutsford chronicles. Not until George II came to the throne in 1727 did this inn—renamed The George in the King's honour —begin to play a real part in the events of the town.

The nobs of Cheshire pooled their resources to build the George's Assembly Hall, a magnificent room with a minstrels' gallery and glittering chandeliers. It quickly became the focal point of the county's social life, throbbing with gaieties, dazzling with young beauties, sparkling with the diamonds adorning the scented womenfolk of the elite of the neighbourhood.

And circulating among them was a man named Edward Higgins, who, says the Rev. Henry Green in his history of Knutsford* 'hunted with them during the morning, dined with them in the afternoon and made himself familiar with their plate-chests by night.'

* *Knutsford: Its Traditions and History*, by Henry Green, A. M. (Smith & Elder, London)

The Royal George, Knutsford (No. 15): the old courtyard

The Royal George: the old coachway

'Edward Higgins, Gent. of Nether Knutsford,' lived in a house on the heath side, then called Cann Office House. 'In a simple rustic neighbourhood,' wrote Henry Green, 'amongst good-natured peasants, for a long time he was regarded with simple curiosity, rather than suspicion; and even the curiosity pointed to his horse more than to himself . . .

'At length, however, a violent suspicion broke loose against him; for it was ascertained that on certain nights, when, perhaps, he had motives for concealing the fact of having been abroad, he drew woollen stockings over his horse's feet, with the purpose of deadening the sound of riding up a brick-paved entry, common to his own stable and that of a respectable neighbour.'

When this clever, even courteous, highwayman went to the gallows on November 7, 1767, he left behind him a wife and five children, a detailed confession of his criminal exploits, including murder, and a ghost that frequents the Round Room of the Royal George. During the Georgian period, this was the powder room and probably the place where Higgins made some of his lushest pickings, slipping in unnoticed at the height of a ball, rifling the trinket boxes and toilet cases, lifting jewellery left pinned to capes and coats, and, if disturbed, hiding himself in the voluminous folds of the window drapes.

There is one delightful story told by Henry Green of how Higgins narrowly escaped being brought to book years earlier than the fateful day when he was eventually arrested in Wales. 'He had been at the county assembly in Knutsford, and had observed how splendidly a Lady Warburton was attired in diamonds and other jewels; in his mind's eye they were all set down as plunder for Cann-Office House. He left the assembly at an early hour and, mounting his horse, took the road towards Arley. After a while the family coach came rolling along, but he passed the carriage instead of attacking it: he then turned back for the assault, and was just about to attempt the robbery, when he was disconcerted by Lady Warburton perceiving him, and saying, "Goodnight! Mr Higgins. Why did you leave the ball so early?" Being thus recognised he gave up the attack, and the lady and her jewels escaped.'

Mr M R Willcocks of Wilson's Brewery in Manchester mentioned another haunting at the Royal George—a phantom coach, with ghostly coachmen, complete with the noise of iron-rimmed wheels on the cobbles and the trumpeting of the posthorn. Unfortunately it has not been possible to find out any more about it. Who knows: perhaps this ghostly arrival was the unsuspecting Lady Warburton intent on a delicious gossip with that nice Mr Higgins?

Cornwall

The Lonely Sailor of Bodmin Moor

16   JAMAICA INN, Bolventor.
A free house on Bodmin Moor, adjacent to the A30, Launceston to Bodmin road. Open : 11 to 2.30 & 5 to 10.30. Sunday : 12 to 2 & 7 to 10. Accommodation available. Snacks at the bar. Ample parking. Nearest station : Bodmin Road. Telephone : Pipers Pool 250.

THERE CANNOT be many who have not heard of this pub since Daphne du Maurier wrapped a novel around it and Hollywood put its own version on celluloid. To get a true picture of Jamaica Inn, however, you must see it on a wild midwinter day when the wind is howling across the grey, deserted landscape, hurling the persistent drizzle at the granite walls with demented fury. Then you can shut out the remaining signs of civilisation, in particular the broad black ribbon of highway which slices through the hundred square miles of monotonous moor, and concentrate on the inn of three centuries back.

In those days there was only the pub. The village of Bolventor—a 'bold venture' indeed—grew up slowly after the 25 miles of cart track linking Launceston with Bodmin was improved sufficiently in the mid-18th century to be called a road. Much to the disgust of the smuggling fraternity.

To them this inn, isolated in the very middle of a lonely, forbidding moorland wilderness, was the ideal location from which to carry on the business of free trading without interference from the law.

By smugglers' pack pony both the north and south coasts of Cornwall were no more than twenty miles away. Once the contraband cargo was ashore it was but a few hours' trek under cover of darkness to the safety of Jamaica Inn. An 'honest' waggoner did the rest, taking it on to other taverners along the road to Falmouth, or Plymouth, or Bristol, even to London.

At the end of the 18th century this emporium of the Cornish free-traders suddenly advanced into the world of legitimate business. A landlord named James Broad, who died in 1803, established it as a posting house, serving the coaches that made the often perilous journey to Falmouth to link with the mail packet boats.

Seamen from these boats, which had been sailing with regularity since 1688, were paid off on arrival at Falmouth after months, sometimes years, at sea. Often they made their way to their homes up-country, usually on foot or cadging a ride with a carrier from inn to inn. One such sailor, drinking in what is now Mary's Bar*, was called by a stranger to attend to business outside in the cobbled yard. He put his half finished pot of ale on the table and went out into the night. In the morning he was found dead on the moor, his money gone.

Though his killer was never discovered, his ghost has been both seen and heard frequently. Many times he has been back to finish that drink, his ghostly footsteps stomping along the passage that leads to Mary's Bar, or moving about upstairs.

In the years immediately before the outbreak of World War I, though fast cars and luxury coaches were the things yet to come, this old smugglers' inn on the moor still drew a sizeable number of sightseers. Some among them were intrigued by the lone figure they noticed sitting on the low wall outside the inn, a man in old-fashioned seaman's clothes, who spoke to nobody and who was never seen to move.

It was the done thing in Edwardian times to write to the Press about any such extraordinary thing as this, which a good many did after witnessing the lonely sailor. The description most people gave of him, both in and out of print, fitted that of the murdered man and it was generally accepted that this was his ghost.

Jamaica Inn has not changed a great deal since then, or for that matter, since it was first built in 1547. The surrounding countryside is not quite the same and the customers are more tolerant of the law, but the pub is basically unaltered—stone-flagged floors, massive fireplaces of granite, oak ceiling beams salvaged from a wrecked ship's timbers. There was a time when it looked as if this once notorious old inn might end its days in sober-sided obscurity. That was in 1893 when it was renamed Bolventor Temperance Hotel, a short-lived state of affairs which must have given its beer-drinking ghost quite a turn.

* So called after Mary Yellan, the heroine in Daphne du Maurier's book *Jamaica Inn*.

Finny the Gook

17 FINNYGOOK INN, Crafthole.
An Ind Coope house on the coast road (B3247) from Torpoint to Looe. Open: 10.30 to 2.30 & 5.30 to 10.30. Sunday: 12 to 2 & 7 to 10.30. Snacks. Parking. Nearest station: St Germans (4 mls.). Telephone: St Germans 338.

ORIGINALLY this pub was known as The New Inn. Three cottages had been knocked into one to form it. It was much used in those days by a freetrader named Finny who headed a gang which landed its contraband on the wide silver-sanded beaches of Whitsand Bay. The revenue men at last intercepted them as they were transferring a cargo from the inn to Plymouth. In the ensuing fight Finny was killed, leaving behind a gook (Cornish for ghost) thought to be responsible for a number of unusual happenings and noises. There have been no such reports in recent years. The inn was renamed The Finnygook in 1950.

The Ghost in a Three-Cornered Hat

18   THE DOLPHIN, The Harbour, Penzance.
A Devenish (Redruth) house, 25 yards from harbour steps. Open : 11 to 2.30 & 5.30 to 10.30. Sunday : 12 to 2 & 7 to 10.30. Snacks at bar. Accommodation. Parking. Nearest station : Penzance. Telephone : Penzance 2560.

WHAT A PLEASURE it is to sup a pint in this pub and do nothing more than contemplate the scene from the front windows. You can just sit looking out past the high-and-dry bell buoys labelled with romantic-sounding names such as Skeeries Bank and Spanish Ledge, to the fairy-tale contours of St Michael's Mount dominating the bay.

If you are not a fisherman and have no need to buy 'fresh bait at the bar' and be gone, you can stay a while longer to light up a pipe of choicest Virginian while watching the Scilly Isles steamer disembark its bronzed cargo of holiday folk.

It may be considered by some a dubious claim to fame, but this was the pub in which Virginian tobacco was first smoked, it being the tavern nearest to the water front. In those far-off Elizabethan days Mounts Bay was jammed with shipping, mostly vessels just back from beyond, that put in briefly to replenish supplies of everything from water to women, and at the Dolphin sea-weary men found all they needed to satisy their thirst and their lust.

One wonders if the ghost that roams the Dolphin—an old sea-faring character, sporting a tricorn hat and lace ruffles, which suggests some-body of rank—is perhaps a captain off one of those ships, who died at the hands of a besotted, sex-crazed crew? Or was he another victim of the bloody Judge Jeffreys, who descended on Cornwall with as much vengeance as anywhere else on the road west. At Penzance he moved into The Dolphin, turning the dining-room into a court and the cellars into a jail, and proceeded to dole out his savage sentences.

Just a hundred years before him Sir John Hawkins, the Elizabethan sailor, had moved into The Dolphin, but for a very different purpose. He made this unpretentious pub the headquarters from which he organised the Cornish contingent of men and ships to fight the Spanish Armada.

There are few Cornish pubs that were not associated with the smuggling business and proof of The Dolphin's connection was

The Dolphin, Penzance (No. 18)

revealed a few years ago when builders discovered a cellar hideaway in which contraband was stored; in fact, two brandy casks in good condition were found there. Further evidence came to light as recently as 1966 after a fire at the inn, when a sealed-up door was uncovered in a bedroom. It led to a small room built into the roof, in which region heavy, measured footsteps have been heard passing from the front to the rear of the building, but never returning. Some think they could be a ghostly re-enactment of the last walk of some mortally wounded smuggler hidden from the Excise men in the sealed room.

The Murdered Girl

19 THE STAR, Truro.
*A St Austell Brewery house in Castle Street. Open: 11 to 2.30 &
5 to 11. Serves meals. Accommodation: 3 double rooms. Car park
nearby. Nearest station: Truro. Telephone: Truro 3028.*

AN OLD coaching house in the Georgian style, once known as The Castle because it stood practically next door to a battlemented stronghold. In its early days it was the scene of a murder of a young girl, whose ghost has been frequently seen haunting in the late evenings.

Friar's Haunt

20 THE WILLIAM THE FOURTH, Truro.
*A St Austell Brewery house in Kenwyn Street. Open: 10.30 to 2.30
& 5.30 to 10.30. Sunday: 12 to 2 & 7 to 10. Snacks at lunch time.
Nearest station: Truro. Telephone: Truro 3334.*

THIS PUB changed its name from The George the Fourth to The William the Fourth when the sailor prince became king. It is built on the site of a Dominican friary which may account for the ghost of a friar which haunts the vicinity.

Derbyshire

Billy the Butcher?

21 CUMBERLAND HEAD HOTEL, Beighton, Derbyshire
A Tennents (of Sheffield) house 6½ miles south-east of Sheffield on B6059. Open: 11 to 3 & 5.30 to 10.30. Sunday: 12 to 2 & 7 to 10.30. Accommodation. Snacks, lunches and dinner. Parking. Nearest station. Sheffield. Telephone: Woodhouse 3454.

THERE CAN BE little doubt that the Cumberland Head is commemorative of the second son of George II, who crushed the Scots at Culloden and earned himself the title 'Billy the Butcher.' If it is his ghost that walks in this pub it must be because of a tormented conscience for allowing his army to act so cruelly after defeating Prince Charlie.

As parts of the house are of 13th-century origin, it is possible the haunting began long before the Duke of Cumberland's rise and fall. Nevertheless, the ghostly misbehaviour at the pub caused a former landlady to vacate her bedroom and sleep elsewhere. 'It sounded just like someone walking across the room,' she said. 'I wouldn't like to have slept there. But,' she added, 'I'm sure he's a friendly ghost.'

Devon

The Taciturn Bishop?

22 BISHOP LACY INN, Chudleigh.
*A Whitbread house on the Exeter to Ashburton road (A38). Open:
10 to 2 & 5 to 10.30. Sunday: 12 to 2 & 7 to 10.30. Snacks. Accommodation. Parking. Nearest station: Newton Abbott. Telephone:
Chudleigh 2196.*

IT WAS a night in 1966, near closing time, when Walter Brown, then
landlord of the Bishop Lacy Inn, was clearing up in the bar.

'Sorry sir, we're just closing,' said Mr Brown to the cloaked figure
that came through the door. But the 'customer' didn't answer and went
on past the bar and up the stairs leading to the bedrooms.

'Hey, you can't go up there,' called Mr Brown; 'that's private.'

He dashed up the stairs after the intruder and met his wife coming
down to see what was the cause of the commotion.

'Someone has just gone upstairs,' he explained, and turned to another
customer to verify his statement.

'That's nonsense,' said his wife. 'No one came up the stairs—except
you.'

After that one-sided conversation with the cloaked figure many
customers at the inn have wondered if it was the ghost of a monk or
possibly of Bishop Lacy himself, since the house was originally a
monastery, and in the 14th century the summer residence of Edmund
Lacy, then Bishop of Exeter.

Regulars have reported 'feeling a presence' about the place; overnight guests have heard inexplicable footsteps. In the late spring of
1968 a couple and their son planned to stay at the 600-years-old pub
for three days, but in the night they heard the ghost walking and left
next morning. Friends of the landlord have heard the footsteps as well
as other strange sounds 'which they tend to take for granted.'

The Bishop Lacy Inn is the oldest building in Chudleigh, it being the
only place to survive a great fire in 1807. It has a wealth of beamed
ceilings, belonging at one time to the monastery chapel. An oak door
in the lounge bar is the entrance to a tunnel under the road which once
connected the house with the church.

The Terrified Barmaid

**23 OLD SMUGGLERS' INN, Coombe Cellars,
near Teignmouth.**

A free house on the south side of the Teignmouth-Shaldon toll-bridge (A379). Open : 10.30 to 2 & 5 to 10.30. Sunday : 12 to 2 & 7 to 10.30. Serves food. Accommodation. Parking. Nearest station : Teignmouth Telephone : Shaldon 2423.

FOR WEEKS a barmaid at this old inn on the banks of the River Teign was convinced she was sharing her bedroom with a ghost. She woke night after night terrified by 'an awful feeling of not being alone,' yet when she complained nobody would take her seriously. That is, not until the proprietor went to an auction and bought up some old prints of the pub. One of them depicted a woman being murdered by an intruder more than a hundred years before in the very room occupied by the terrified barmaid . . .

The Phantom Coach

24 ROYAL CASTLE, The Quay, Dartmouth.

A Courage Barclay house. Open : 10.30 to 2.30 & 5.30 to 10.30 (Fri. & Sat. 11). June 1st to September 30th closing time is 11 every night. Lunches and dinner. Accommodation (26 bedrooms). Parking opposite or close by in corporation park. Nearest station : Kingswear. Telephone : Dartmouth 2525.

DARTMOUTH is a gem of a town, clustered below a steep hillside of the Dart Valley. It earned itself a name in history when Richard Coeur de Lion set sail from there to distinguish himself as a Crusader. There was no Royal Castle then, probably just a riverside cottage displaying the sign of the evergreen bush and supplying food and drink to passing travellers, mostly merchants and seamen from Plymouth or Brixham.

There can be little doubt that the present place is old, even older than the year 1639 engraved on the plaque above the crooked doorway. Handhewn timber salvaged 50 years earlier from one of the Spanish ships of the routed Armada washed up three miles away on Blackpool Sands, went into the building of the original harbour tavern.

Drake once stayed here and has a bedroom, complete with four-poster bed, named after him. Charles II, Queen Victoria and Edward VII came too. In fact, seven reigning monarchs have enjoyed the hospitality of this comfortable, mellowed, ever-welcoming quayside inn—where you can lie abed and hear the water lapping against the landing stage.

Edward VII, who indulged in the good things of life, not least his food, made public his appreciation of the Royal Castle by scratching his initials on a mirror with a diamond ring he was wearing. Royalty before him—William and Mary of Orange—left behind a more dramatic

The Royal Castle, Dartmouth (No. 24)

reminder, a phantom coach and horses, described by a visitor who saw them as 'three flea-bitten greys and an odd coloured bay on the outside left.'

It is more usual to see nothing, but to waken in the night to the sound of a galloping horseman and later to hear the ringing clatter of several horses pulling a coach over the cobbles into what is now the hall of the hotel. There are footsteps. The coach doors are opened and slammed shut. The team is whipped up and the coach rumbles off into the night at speed. A church clock, seemingly in the silent street behind the hotel, strikes two . . .

This haunting happens only in the autumn, between September and November. It coincides with the anniversary of the arrival in Devon of William and Mary to accept the English throne. William, with an army of 15,000 Dutchmen, planned originally to land at Dartmouth in the autumn of 1688, but a Channel storm and the possibility of an unenthusiastic reception decided him to put into Torbay. Princess Mary, a poor sailor, had made the crossing earlier and awaited her husband at the Royal Castle which, at that time, was two pairs of houses face to face across a narrow roadway, which gave access to coaches.

News of Prince William's change of plan was delivered to Mary in the early hours by a special courier who rode by way of Totnes Bridge to warn her that a coach was on its way to take her urgently to Brixham. It arrived in fact shortly before 2 am.

For 20 years Mrs Gwyneth Powell has lived with this phantom coach. She is manageress of the Royal Castle. 'I have never ever seen anything,' she says, 'but I've heard the coach many times. It has always been followed by the clock striking 2 o'clock in the morning. It's strange that although it is always on time, it's not regular by date, which may have something to do with the change of the calendar over the years.'

The Placid Spirit

25 COWICK BARTON INN, Cowick Lane, Exeter.
A Courage house. Open: 10.30 to 2 & 5 to 10.30. Sunday: 12 to 2 & 7 to 10.30. Nearest station: Exeter. Telephone: Exeter 75623.

UNTIL 1963 this was a 400-year-old farmhouse fast falling into ruins. Courage, Barclay and Simmonds took it over and transformed it into Exeter's newest pub complete with its own ghost—a ghost said to be the 'placid spirit' of a monk from the priory which occupied the site before the farmhouse stood there.

The Vacant Chair and the Lovelorn Monk

26 THE PIG AND WHISTLE, Littlehempston, Totnes.
A free house on the A381 Totnes-to-Newton Abbot road. Open:
10.30 to 2.30 & 5.30 to 10.30 including Sundays. Snacks at the bar.
Self-contained flat available. Nearest station: Totnes (2 mls.).
Telephone: Totnes 2324.

THERE IS a vacant fireside chair in the bar of the Pig and Whistle reserved for the ghost, a hunch-backed monk with a smiling face, who is said to make a dramatic entrance through a window where once there was a door.

Few have seen him, but many have heard and seen the window swing open without cause and assume that Freddie—as the regulars call him—has arrived. Odd that they should call him Freddie, since he is believed to be the ghost of Brother Joseph, a monk of French origin from the old Abbey at Buckfast, some six or seven miles to the west.

The history of this 400-years-old pub is vague but there is a suggestion that it was once a lodging house for the brethren and pilgrims travelling the road from the coast to Buckfast. The building adjoining was a chapel and the two are connected by a tunnel. A similar tunnel leads to a near-by quarry from which the stone to build both places was cut.

The Atmosphere In The Bar

In the absence of the facts a story, embroidered by repetition, has grown up around Brother Joseph, telling of his love for a woman who wandered the lanes of Littlehempston soliciting the farm hands as they worked in the fields. Almost every day the hunch-backed monk would ride over to meet her at the inn, leaving his horse tied up outside the well-house and entering the inn by way of the door that has since been removed.

If disturbed in his love-making he would leave through the tunnel into the adjoining chapel and emerge nonchalantly into the daylight, telling his beads.

Apart from the unexplained sudden opening of doors and windows, the landlady has other evidence of the ghost. She recalls: 'I hate being in the bar by myself after dark. It is difficult to explain, but there is a strange atmosphere in the place. One evening a man and woman from Plymouth stopped for a drink and as they were leaving the woman told me that her husband, who was clairvoyant, had seen the figure of a monk following me around the bar. It's a bit uncanny.'

Old Abe and the Sad-faced Cavalier

27 WHO'D HAVE THOUGHT IT. Milton Coombe, near Yelverton.

A free house a few miles west of the Plymouth to Yelverton road. Open: 10.30 to 2.30 & 5.30 to 10.30. Friday & Saturday: 5.30 to 11. Sunday: 12 to 2 & 7 to 10.30. Accommodation. Snacks at bar. Parking. Nearest station: Plymouth. Telephone: Yelverton 3313.

THIS WAS Sir Francis Drake's local. He lived a five-minute gallop away at Buckland Abbey on the edge of Dartmoor. In this part of Devon one can still hear from the lips of old countrymen the story of the shepherd who was searching the rugged countryside for straying sheep when he came upon the body of a sailor lying in the shelter of a hollow. The sailor was fully clothed and his head rested on a bundle he had been carrying. There was a little dog curled up at his feet. Both man and dog had obviously lost their way and had lain down, exhausted, to rest. When the shepherd found them months later they were skeletons.

It is not surprising that this 16th-century inn in this lonely valley was once called The Welcome which indeed it must have been for travellers after they had made the perilous crossing of the moor on foot.

In those distant days there was another pub in the village—where the post office and general store is today—which was called The First and Last Inn—again a name chosen with the welfare of the moorland traveller in mind.

The First and Last was by far the more popular of the two inns, though like The Welcome it was licensed to sell only beer and cider. When the landlord of one decided it was time he applied for a licence to sell wines and spirits, the other landlord felt compelled to follow suit.

But the unexpected happened. The spirits licence was granted to the landlord of The Welcome. Waving the vital document he rushed excitedly into the street where a crowd of villagers yelled in amazement 'Who'd ha' thought it?' From then on they referred to The Welcome as The Who'd Have Thought It and very soon that was the only name by which it was known.

The inn sign, a massive painting in oils by Alan Bowyer, depicts the successful landlord confronting the crowd. But he is not the landlord whose ghost haunts this inn. That is Abe Beer, a previous licensee well remembered in the valley of Milton Coombe, who made his ghostly presence felt from the very first night the new landlord and his wife moved in.

The ghost of 'Old Abe' does not haunt alone. There is a phantom cavalier, described as 'sad-faced with chestnut hair falling to his shoulders and dressed in a wine-coloured topcoat.' He has been seen sitting on the end of a bed, from time to time, but no one has yet been able to decide which of the two—Old Abe or the cavalier—it is who rings the service bell in the bar. When answered the bell pull is still swinging but there is nobody waiting for attention.

The Noisy Silence

28 CHURCH HOUSE INN, Torbryan, near Newton Abbott.
A Tolchard house 1½ miles west of the A381, Newton Abbott to Totnes road. Lunches and dinner. Snacks at bar. Open : 11 to 2.30 & 6 to 10.30. Friday & Saturday to 11. Sunday : 12 to 2 & 7 to 10.30. Parking. Nearest station : Newton Abbott. Telephone : Ipplepen 372.

WHEN MICK HEAP moved into Church House Inn early in 1966 he tried to forget the strange things the previous landlord had told him.

'Only people who are standing up and breathing can do you any harm. The dead can't harm you,' he told himself. But when Chris Barrett of *The South Devon Journal* called on him in the summer of '68, he was not quite so sceptical. There had been one or two curious happenings that tempted him to change his mind about ghosts.

'One night when I was locking up I came into the bar with my dog Tina,' he told Mr Barrett. 'Smoky, the cat, was sitting just inside the bar. Suddenly Tina's hackles rose and Smoky arched her back. They were both staring at something in the corner. I could not see anything myself but I had a strange feeling. Then the cat shot up the stairs like a rocket. She had never been upstairs before. After that, for a long time, Tina used to stand on the landing every night at precisely the same hour, and bark. When I went up to see if anyone was there I found nobody.'

The previous tenants of this moorside pub, like Mick Heap, never actually saw a ghost, but they were troubled by noises, footsteps clumping along the landing to the bathroom, late at night.

There was the time when the landlord had gone to a New Year's Eve party, leaving his mother and father to look after the pub. At midnight, as they lay awake to welcome in the New Year, the door at the bottom of the staircase creaked open and footsteps came thumping up the stairs.

As the steps went past their room they called out 'Happy New Year! You're home early: It must have been a rotten party.' They thought no more about it and went to sleep—only to be roused again at 5 o'clock when their son really did arrive home.

*　　　*　　　*

But the RAF man who slept the night by the bar-room fire, when there was no accommodation elsewhere, saw the ghost when he woke in the early hours 'aware of something odd.' As his eyes became accustomed to the glow from the dying embers, he saw the sitting figure of a monk on the other side of the room. As he went towards it, the image seemed to melt into the panelled wall.

Perhaps the village policeman also saw the ghost the day he called to introduce himself, being new to the district and wanting to meet the locals. While talking to the landlord in the bar he looked round and asked, 'Who's the old man sitting over there?'

'There was nobody,' the landlord said, 'though the policeman swore he saw someone.'

And a visiting Canadian woman once refused to walk along the upstairs landing because she swore there was 'a presence' there.

Like so many pubs with this name, the Church House Inn was originally a cottage built to provide food and lodging for the masons and monks working on the near-by church. Not two miles away across the moor at Broadhempston is another Church House Inn which had its beginnings in much the same way and claims to be haunted—by a smell, the sweet smell of incense, which wafts through the building, particularly at Easter and Christmastime.

When Chris Barrett went to see this landlord, he said: 'The first time I smelled it I asked my home help about it and she said it seemed as though something was burning. She thought it was lavender. We tried to trace the source but we couldn't find it. There was no smoke. Just this very sweet smell. It is strongest in my bedroom. You get used to the smell of beer and stale tobacco in a pub, but this is really quite pleasant.

'Quite often Measles (his Dalmatian) growls and sniffs around for no apparent reason, but I am quite used to that now. There is obviously nothing harmful here,' he said, adding: 'I really enjoy living in this place, it is so completely serene. I never realised night was so black and silence so noisy.'

The Phantom Hound

29 BLACK DOG HOTEL, Uplyme.
A Palmers (of Bridport) house on the A3070 road from Lyme Regis to Axminster. Open : 10.30 to 2.30 & 5.30 to 10.30. Sunday : 12 to 2 & 7 to 10.30. Limited accommodation. Lunch and dinner. Snacks at bar. Nearest station : Axminster. Telephone : Lyme Regis 2634.

WHEN Sir Arthur Conan Doyle heard about the spectral Black Dog of Devon he wrote a Sherlock Holmes who-dunnit about the animal and called it *The Hound of the Baskervilles.*

Elsewhere it gets called by other names. In Suffolk it is the Galley Trot, in Norfolk Black Shuck, in Lancashire Shriker, in Yorkshire Padfoot. It originated with the Vikings from the legend of the Hound of Odin, which the Saxons called Scucca (Shuck), the Devil.

Doyle's dog, it is generally supposed, was based on the Black Dog of Torrington, a snarling, baying monster with blazing eyes like the lenses of a lantern. By comparison, the Black Dog of Uplyme is a gentle ghost, though the old inn sign painted above the door of this pub used to portray it as a black fiend, a grotesque and horrible creature. Its adoption as the name and sign for the inn arose from this legend, which I quote from *The Bridport News,* a local Dorset newspaper: 'An old farmer lived in part of a demolished mansion—it was next door to the inn—the building was frequented by the ghost of a black dog, which sat with the farmer by the fireside at night. The old man grew accustomed to the spectre but his neighbours used to tell him to rid himself of the apparition. The farmer, however, refused, saying the dog was the quietest thing in the house and it ate nothing.

'One night the farmer went out drinking with a neighbour, who taunted him about the dog. Excited by the other man's words, the farmer determined to do away with the dog. He went home and seized a poker and advanced towards the black animal. The dog, realising his intention, jumped from its seat and rushed off to an attic. The drunken man swayed after it. He entered the attic in time to see the dog disappear through the ceiling. Angrily he struck the spot where the dog had stood. To his amazement a small box fell from the ceiling. The farmer opened it and discovered a large sum in gold and silver coins of Charles I's reign.

'The dog was never seen in the house again, but, until this very day, it continues to haunt, at midnight, the lane which leads to the house.'

In their *History of Signboards* (Chatto & Windus), Larwood and Hotten give the story a shade more credibility. They made the point that the house in which the farmer lived was formerly a Royalist mansion largely destroyed by Cromwell's army, which could account for the conceal- ment of a large sum of gold and silver coins in the roof timbers, out of sight of Roundhead eyes and dislodged by the farmer when mending the hole in the roof the next day.

They mention too that the lane which leads to the pub is now the favourite haunt of the spectral hound and was named Dog Lane in consequence.

'Harry' and the Weeping Child

30 THE OLD INN, Widecombe-in-the-Moor.
A free house on Dartmoor about three miles north of the A384 at Poundsgate. Open : 11 to 2.30 & 6 to 10.30. June to September open to 11. Sunday : 12 to 2 & 7 to 10.30. Snacks. No accommodation. Nearest station : Newton Abbott. Telephone : Widecombe 207.

UNCLE TOM COBLEIGH and his cronies downed a gill or two at this pub before returning from the fair on the sagging back of Tom Pearse's old grey work horse. Their excursion, immortalised in song and fable, has done more to make Widecombe known the world over than any jet-age tourist gimmick ever could.

Go into the Old Inn on any fine summer Sunday and you can hear at least half a dozen different foreign tongues wagging at once. There's almost sure to be one talking about 'Harry,' the ghost that has been seen walking in mid-afternoon from the main kitchen into the adjoining smaller one, from which there is no exit. He is a solid-looking figure— 'nothing hazy or whispy about him,' who invariably walks in the same direction and then just fades away. Harry is not alone in his haunt. There is also the ghost of a crying child.

Several times sudden violent sobbing has been heard, but the bedroom from which the crying comes is always found to be empty.

'A fitful, heartrending sob' is how a former landlord's wife once described it. 'It always comes from the same room,' she said. 'We've checked time and time again but there is never anyone there.'

It would be strange to talk about ghosts in the bar of The Old Inn and not hear about Mary Jay whose lonely grave one passes on the road across the moor, about two miles north of the village. A tiny black speck on the map marks JAY'S GRAVE, below Bonehill Down, the spot where Widecombe folk of a hundred years back buried Mary: she had committed suicide to avoid the shame of bearing her lover's child.

It is not Mary's ghost they will tell you about in the pub, but the ghost of a stooping figure that is sometimes seen at the graveside, a dark blanket over head and shoulders, obscuring the face. That, they say, could explain the bunch of fresh wild flowers that has been left lying on the overgrown mound over the years.

DEVIL'S FOOTNOTE: On Sunday, October 21, 1638, disaster struck Widecombe. *The Guinness Book of Records* says it was a tornado that swept through the village, wrecking the church, killing four of the afternoon congregation and injuring 62. However, the people of 17th-century Widecombe were convinced it was the Devil who rode through their village. They were all the more certain because of an incident that happened the same afternoon three miles away at The Tavistock Inn, in Poundsgate. A stranger riding a coal-black horse called at the inn and asked the way to Widecombe. The innkeeper's wife directed him and brought him a pot of ale, which, so the story goes, hissed and spluttered as he gulped it down. He threw some coins on the counter, walked out without a word and leapt into the saddle, leaving the woman in no doubt that she had served the Devil himself.

Dorset

The Phantom Pianist

31 CROWN HOTEL, Poole.
An Elridge Pope house in Market Street in the town centre. Open:
10 to 2.30 & 6 to 11. Sunday: 12 to 2 & 7 to 10.30. Nearest station:
Poole. Telephone: Poole 2137.

A LONE NOTE played on a piano by an unseen hand, the sound of a
body being dragged along the floor, a vague fluorescent shape moving
down a staircase; these are the paranormal happenings that, in 1966,
led Mr D Browne, an Australian staying at this inn, to conduct experi-
ments to disprove the haunting. But the ghost won and Mr Browne
later described his experience as 'the most eerie I have ever had in my
life.' The Crown's landlord said the haunting began when the builders
started to convert outbuildings into a club for beat music.

Co. Durham

A 'Regular' Still?

32 ALBION INN, Bill Quay, near Gateshead.
A Bass Charrington house at Felling 3 miles east of Gateshead on A184. Open: 11 to 3 & 5.30 to 10.30. Sunday: 12 to 2 & 7 to 10.30. Snacks at bar. Nearest station: Felling (via Newcastle). Telephone: Felling 692418.

WHEN OLD Charlie Gordon died a few years ago a whole neighbourhood mourned the passing of the man they all knew as 'the gentleman of Bill Quay.' He was a regular at the Albion for a lifetime, having looked in almost every day for sixty years, since he was a lad in his late teens. Mrs Lucy Stanborough had been landlady at this pub for only two weeks when she met Charlie—as a ghost. She saw him sitting at the bar shortly before evening opening time, a tall man in a grey suit and a black Homburg hat. As she approached he faded away, though she saw him again several times after that, standing near the serving hatch. Present-day regular customers told Mrs Stanborough, who never knew Charlie Gordon when he was alive, that her description fitted him perfectly. 'I was startled at first. Now I'm not frightened at all,' says Mrs Stanborough. 'Everyone says he was a very kind man who wouldn't harm a soul. He must have really liked it here.'

A Pint for the Ghost

33 THE MARINE GROTTO, Marsden, near Sunderland.
A Vaux Breweries house on the South Shields to Sunderland Cliff road (A183). Open: 11 to 3 & 6 to 10. Sunday: 12 to 2 & 7 to 10. Lunch and dinner. No accommodation. Parking on cliff top. Nearest station: South Shields. Telephone: South Shields 4055 or 2043.

IF JACK THE BLASTER could see Marsden Grotto today he wouldn't believe his eyes. The cave he blasted out of the limestone cliff to make a home for himself and his wife in 1782 has been transformed into a show-

An old photograph of the Marine Grotto, Marsden (No. 33)

piece inn, unique in seaside England—and haunted too, though not by Jack.

The rough-hewn cavern in which Jack's wife served simple refreshments to sightseers from 18th-century South Shields and Sunderland has long since been supplanted by a long, low, white-painted hotel squatting at the foot of the 100 ft. cliff, its wide windows looking out over a broad terrace towards the bird island of Marsden Rock.

Dominating it all—and this is what Jack or his returning ghost would notice long before anything else—is the concrete tower of the 'observation' lift which, in forty seconds, can whisk one up or down the cliff face, with a spectacular view en route.

Although Jack the Blaster died in 1792 a comparatively wealthy man from catering for the curious, it was Peter Allan, son of a local gamekeeper, who saw the potential for making real money from the Grotto. Peter was a powerfully built bushy-bearded man in his mid-twenties. He moved into the one-roomed cave some thirty years after Jack's death and began to dig his way farther and farther into the cliff. He excavated eight separate chambers, as well as uncovering eighteen skeletons, supposedly bodies of smugglers killed in action.

Spiced Buns and Singin' Hinnies

With rock displaced by his massive excavations Peter made a wide raised promenade on the beach in front of the cave entrance. On this substantial foundation he built two white-washed cottages backing on to the cliffs. Here the man the locals nicknamed Peter the Hermit lived with his wife and reared a family of eight children, while catering for summer pleasure seekers. Mrs Allan's spiced buns and singin' hinnies were as much the talk of County Durham as the Grotto itself.

When some years later Peter the Hermit was granted an ale and spirit licence despite opposition from suspicious Excise men, he drove a shaft upwards from one of the caves south of the Grotto to the top of the cliffs, to give easier access for his barrels. Used in reverse, the local smugglers found it a god-send for disposing of cargoes of contraband shipped into Marsden Bay.

And ship them they did until John the Jibber, a member of the Marsden gang, betrayed them to the coastguards, who lay in wait one night to seize a shipload of tobacco, and the men who had smuggled it. But someone—maybe it was Peter the Hermit—sensing treachery, let off his pistol, which set the dogs barking and warned the skipper of the smugglers' lugger lying offshore. When the coastguards searched the Grotto there were a large number of tough-looking, hard-drinking men, dancing to the music of a fiddle and a concertina—but no sign of illicit tobacco.

When the gang eventually caught John the Jibber they did not wait to hear his story but trussed him up and hoisted him in a tub on the end of a rope halfway up the Smugglers' Hole.

Chamber's Journal, reporting the story some time later, says he was 'let down once a day to receive some scant food and the gibes of his mates, his situation being rendered yet more cruel from his position permitting him to witness his comrades feasting and being made a target for the refuse of their festivities.'

Eventually he was left to die hanging in the tub high up in the Grotto shaft, his piteous groans for help echoing through the caverns. Long after the shaft had collapsed the moans were reported, and for years no one would approach the cave entrance after dark.

More recently there have been other happenings that suggest that the Grotto is haunted. Successive tenants and managers confirm the curious case of the emptied tankard which was first reported many years ago. A landlord was drawing off a pint of ale, when he heard a strange noise. He went to investigate, leaving the full tankard on the bar. On his return the pewter pot was empty although the bar was deserted. Since that day a full tankard, always the same one, is left on the bar at closing time, and various managers over the years confirm that it is found empty each morning.

Mrs Margaret Middleton, the manageress in 1965, tells a story which adds another dimension to the ghostlore of the Grotto. 'My husband saw the ghost through the window of one of our rooms,' she said. 'When he went to investigate the room was empty. No one was there. He went back to our flat in the Grotto, looked out of the sitting-room window and could still see the ghost reflected in the glass.'

Who is this ghost? Was it the man whose skeleton Peter the Hermit found during his big dig, with a flattened lead pistol shot embedded in the dead man's ribs? Or perhaps it was one of the other seventeen skeletons he unearthed, most of whom showed signs of having met violent ends? It is more than likely to be the ghost of Peter Allan himself, who died of a broken heart after being told that the Grotto he'd created with his own bare hands, with his own sweat and blood, was not his.

In 1848, the owners of adjoining property claimed that it was their land and asked Peter for rent. Having had possession for so long Peter said he would never give it up 'so long as he could wag a leg.' At the end of a two-year legal battle Peter was told he could have the Grotto on lease for 20 years at £10 a year. He was told also he would have to pay £50 costs because he had lost the case. He took to his bed on hearing the result and died a few days later on 31st August, 1850, aged 51.

Old Ada Returns

34 THE CROWTREE, Sunderland.
A Vaux Breweries house on corner of Crowtree Street and Park Street. Open: 11 to 3 & 5.30 to 10.30. Sunday: 12 to 2 & 7 to 10.30. Nearest station: Sunderland. Telephone: Sunderland 77748.

FOR MORE THAN 30 years Mrs Ada Holmes pulled pints behind the bar of The Crowtree in Sunderland town centre. Her customers loved her like a mother and when she died in 1965, aged 86, the Parish Church along the road was filled with regulars saying their last goodbye to this frail old lady, whom many had known half a lifetime.

But old Ada couldn't for long keep away from the pub that was her world. A little grey-haired, bespectacled woman, wearing—as Ada invariably did—a multi-coloured dress with a shawl or cardigan, has been seen by the new licensee and family. She watched them playing dominoes one night after closing time and, on another visit, looked at the children lying in bed.

'When we first saw her we could see right through her,' said Mrs Madaliene Thwaites, the landlady, 'but she became more solid until it was just like another person in the room.'

Essex

Wings of Change

35   THE ANGEL, Braintree.
*A Bass Charrington house in Notley Road. Open: 10 to 2.30 &
6 to 10.30. (Friday & Saturday to 11.) Sunday: 12 to 2 & 7 to 10.30.
Snacks at the bar. Parking. Nearest station: Braintree. Telephone:
Braintree 1322.*

THE SIGN swinging over the door of this pub is not everybody's idea
of an angel. This winged female sits astride a high explosive bomb*
and holds aloft a brimming pint tankard, above which hovers a halo.
To this an earthly host reacted with letters to the Press declaring it to
be in bad taste.

When a ghost began to haunt the 400-year-old inn some suggested
that might be due to the installation of the new pub sign. They pointed
out that a local legend says that a former publican of the Angel ex-
pressed a deathbed wish that his inn should not be altered in any way.

It is undeniable that since Mr Len Brookfield became landlord in 1962
there have been many alterations to the old pub, apart from the change
of sign. It's also undeniable that the ghost has appeared regularly since
the builders made the changes. Three big guard-dogs—two normally
fearless boxers and a collie—are terrified by the ghost. Late at night
they howl and bark and wake their master, who finds them shaking with
fright, their hair bristling.

'I've never seen anything but some strange things happen here,' says
Mr Brookfield. 'When the dogs wake me I find that doors I've closed
are open, bottles and glasses have been moved and lights which were
off when we went to bed are on again. Ghosts don't worry me or my
wife. Until now I never believed in them, and this one seems to be
quite harmless. It does not interfere with the beer and it certainly does
not drive customers away.'

* Why a bomb? Because the Angel had a narrow escape during World War
II when the Luftwaffe dropped a delayed action high explosive bomb in the
road outside.

The Boy Martyr

36 THE SWAN, Brentwood.
*An Ind Coope house in the High Street. Open: 10 to 2 & 6 to 10.
Sunday: 12 to 2 & 7 to 10. Lunches. Parking. Nearest station:
Brentwood. Telephone: Brentwood 1848.*

IN BRENTWOOD town centre there is a memorial to William Hunter. Few of the thousands who pass it each day give a second thought as to who he was and why he is commemorated by this obelisk. However, in the 500-year-old Swan Inn, along the High Street, you may be lucky enough to meet somebody who can give you chapter and verse about this Essex martyr. It was at the inn that he spent his last days before going to the stake, and it is there his ghost is said to walk.

William was only a boy of 19 when he was burned for his Protestant beliefs. That was on the morning of March 26, 1555, after his last night at The Swan during which, in the early hours of the morning, he had a dream about his execution, all of which happened in much the way he foresaw it.

His brother, in his account of the martyrdom, describes the final scene in these words:

'Then William Hunter plucked up his gown and stepped over the parlour groundsel and went forward cheerfully . . . And thus going he met with his father according to his dream, and he spake to his son, weeping and saying, "God be with you son William." . . . So William went to the place where the stake stood, even according to his dream, where all things were very unready.

'Then William took a wet broom-faggot and kneeled down thereon and read the fifty-first Psalm . . . Then said the Sherriff, "Here is a letter from the Queen. If thou wilt recant thou shalt live, if not thou shalt be burned."

' "No quoth William, "I shall not recant, God willing."

'Then William rose and went to the stake, and stood upright against it. Then came one, Richard Ponde, a bailif and made fast the chain about William . . . Then said William, "Son of God shine upon me"; and immediately the sun in the element shone out of a dark cloud so full in his face that he was constrained to look another way; whereat the people mused, because it was so dark a little time afore.

'Then William took up a faggot of broom and embraced it in his arms. Then the priest which William had dreamed of, came to his brother, Robert, with a popish book to carry to William that he might recant; which book his brother would not meddle withal . . . William, seeing the priest, and perceiving how he would have showed him the book, said, "Away thou false prophet!"

'Then there was a gentleman which said "I pray God have mercy upon his soul." The people said "Amen, Amen." Immediately fire was made.'

William was one of at least 300 heretics condemned to death during the five years Mary Tudor was on the throne. On the same day as he died another of the five Essex men who were condemned with him, was burned at near-by Horndon on the Hill. By the month's end all had paid the price for their religious convictions and the stench of burning flesh hung like a cloud over that part of the county.

Only William, who probably died from suffocation through the dense smoke from the wet faggots and green reeds, has returned to haunt. His ghost 'has been known to make nightly visits to the inn where he had his premonitory dream' says the daughter of a former licensee. Furthermore, plates bearing religious inscriptions will not stay for long hanging on the pub walls. During the night they are thrown to the floor. Similarly, furniture is mysteriously moved and lights switched on. A dog kept by one landlord refused to go into certain of the rooms and reacted to the ghostly visits with prolonged howling.

The Witch of St Anne's

**37 YE OLD ST ANNE'S CASTLE, Great Leighs,
near Chelmsford.**
An Ind Coope house a mile and half east of the Little Waltham to Braintree road (A131). Open: 10 to 2.30 & 6 to 10.30. Friday & Saturday to 11. Sunday: 12 to 2 & 7 to 10.30. Snacks at bar. Parking. Nearest station: Chelmsford. Telephone: Great Leighs 253.

ST ANNE'S claims to be the oldest hostelry in England. At one time it was a hermitage. After the murder of Becket at Canterbury in 1170 it became a good pull-in for pilgrims on their way to visit the martyr's shrine; here they could stop the night before moving on to cross the Thames at Grays.

One of the bedrooms of the inn is haunted, reputedly by the Witch of Great Leighs, who was burned at the stake in the Middle Ages. During World War II, bulldozers levelling land for an airfield on the outskirts of Great Leighs uncovered the witch's grave. Her bones and the charred faggots of her funeral pyre were found under a boulder not far from the inn. Her ghost is said to have terrorised the village until the remains were reburied near the village cross-roads.

The folk of Great Leighs have vivid memories of those war-time days when their village world turned upside down. These are some of the things that they recall:

- the clock on the parish church chimed backwards;
- hens in the district stopped laying and squawked at night;
- geese disappeared without trace;
- haystacks collapsed without cause.

Meanwhile, back at the pub, equally strange things were happening. The landlord of that time found his bedroom wrecked. Clothes were strewn about the floor, the wardrobe had been moved and a chest of drawers overturned. It looked for all the world like the work of a burglar

Ye Old St Anne's Castle, Great Leighs (No. 37)

except nothing was missing. And when he tidied the room, it happened again! And then again! Each time it happened the landlord was on the premises, serving behind the bar, yet heard no sound from the floor above.

Although the present landlord does not believe in ghosts, his wife does. Says she: 'I won't go into the haunted bedroom. It's evil. I'll tell you another thing too. I won't let anyone sleep in it either.'

Their Alsatian bitch will not stop in the room. If pulled inside on a lead, her fur rises on her neck and she whines and agitates to get out.

But this bedroom with its stately fourposter bed is not the only haunted spot in Ye Old St Anne's Castle. Regulars tell of an old man and woman seen in the car park, who fade away when approached. They talk too of a vague shape of an old man with a ginger beard seen sometimes standing by the fireplace in one of the pub's bars. A most recent incident reported is of an 18-year-old girl, who had not been in the pub before, who screamed as she passed by the fireplace. She said she had seen a man appear beside the chimney. But there was no man there.

Footsteps on Christmas Eve

38 CROSS KEYS HOTEL, High Street, Saffron Walden.
An Ind Coope house in the town centre. Open: 10 to 2.30 & 6 to 10.30. Serves food. Accommodation: five doubles. Nearest station: Audley End. Telephone: Saffron Walden 2207.

SAFFRON WALDEN was Oliver Cromwell's headquarters. At the inn now called the Cross Keys Roundheads drank to the defeat of the Cavaliers and to the success of the man they had helped to make the dictator of all England. An entry in an old account book in the possession of Saffron Walden Corporation reads: '1656, Paid for wine, bread and beer when my Lord Protector was Proclaimed, £2. 16s.'

The inn was called The Whalebone in Cromwell's day—and 200 years before that; it was renamed 100 years after his death. It is now one of the finest timbered inns in East Anglia; it was built originally around a living tree.

The ghost that haunts the narrow corridors and twisting stairways is a Christmas visitant, well documented. The present landlord says: 'Around about Christmas, usually between 11 o'clock and midnight, very heavy, slow, ponderous footsteps are heard from upstairs. Always they go only in one direction—along a corridor which has a blind end.'

The landlord's brother-in-law says: 'The incident, to the best of my memory occurred at exactly midnight on Christmas Eve 1964. I had just begun shutting the door to the side entrance, when I heard heavy footsteps crossing above me in a diagonal direction. They were so heavy as to make the ceiling creak . . . my son rushed up the stairs to see if there was an intruder there. He came down very shortly, having examined the flat and the bedrooms and told me there was nobody.'

A third independent report about the happenings at Christmas 1963 between 11.30 and 11.45 comes from another guest:

'The footsteps were very heavy, and moving along the upper passage-way in the direction of the bathroom. I am not an imaginative man, and have taken such steps as I can conceive to find an explanation; but I know I have heard noises, similar to very heavy and ponderous foot-steps, pass along the upper passage of the Cross Keys, moving away from the stairway towards the deadend, and that on each occasion an immediate and thorough search proved that no living person could have caused them.'

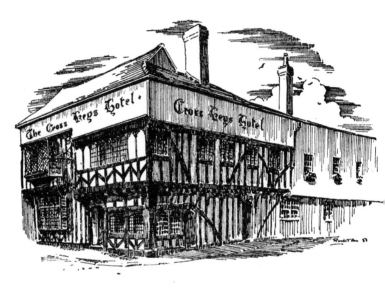

The Cross Keys Hotel, Saffron Walden (No. 38)

The Phantom Bell Ringer

39 THE WHITE HORSE, Sible Hedingham, near Halstead.
A Greene, King & Sons house in Church Street, a mile west of the Halstead to Haverhill road (A132). Open: 10 to 2.30 & 6 to 10.30. Sunday: 12 to 2.30 & 7 to 10.30. Sandwiches at the bar. No accommodation. Parking. Nearest station: Braintree. Telephone. Hedingham 742.

A 15TH-CENTURY pub this, the oldest in the village, reclining behind a white picket fence, a lofty oak shading its mellowed roof. Until the turn of the last century the landlord brewed his own beer and in the yard behind the pub is a cast iron pump from which the brewing water was drawn.

Mrs Wheeler, who lives in a neat, new bungalow, a few hundred yards from the pub was for twenty years its manageress. She took over the White Horse from her father, having come there as a girl. She, better than anybody, knows about the haunting.

'I well remember the first time the ghost rang the front door bell,' says Mrs Wheeler. 'It was snowing hard outside and settling. The bell, one of three old iron ones which worked by pulling on a knob at the front door, rang in the back room and I asked my son-in-law to see who it was. My daughter and her husband, with their son—he was six then—were staying with us, having just come back from Australia. When he came back into the room he said there was nobody at the door. What's more there were no footprints in the snow on the path leading from the front gate.

'After that the bell rang many times and there was never anybody there. Often at night we'd get out of bed because the bell rang but when we looked out of the window over the front door there wasn't a soul. It wasn't the wind or rats, because I saw the bell ringing of its own accord as I was standing below it. Yet no one was at the door pulling the knob. Nobody we could see, that is.

'One night we heard footsteps moving about upstairs and two or three of the customers in the bar dashed up to see who it was. Nobody was up there to my knowledge and they found nothing, nobody. Some evenings when I ran out of change in the bar, I'd go upstairs to get money from a bedroom and often on the stairs I'd feel something brush past me. There were times when I'd feel the same thing as I went into the bedroom. Somebody would brush past me coming out as I went in. But I never saw anything, only the bell clanging.'

Spider up the Chimney

40 THE BEAR INN, Stock.
An Ind Coope house on the Billericay to Chelmsford road (B1007).
Open: 11 to 2.30 & 6 to 10.30. Friday & Saturday to 11. Sunday:
12 to 2 & 7 to 10.30. Sandwiches at bar. Parking. Nearest station:
Chelmsford. Telephone: Stock 232.

THE SPIDER CLUB is one of the most unique clubs in all England. Its membership is exclusive to a dozen men of Essex who, once a year, sit down at a table laden with food and drink to celebrate the existence of a ghost.

This is the ghost of Spider Marshall, who at the turn of the century was the ostler at The Bear Inn, a white-painted country pub with gables and tall Tudor chimneys and best part of 400 years of history under its mossy roof.

This pub is one of the favourites of author and journalist James Wentworth Day, a true countryman, who writes in a delightful way about country things and country people and believes whole-heartedly in ghosts. He lives a mile or two along the road from Stock, knows the landlord, Dick Wheston, like a brother, and is one of the exclusive twelve entitled to membership of the Spider Club.

'Spider has gone but in many ways is with us still. The most enduring legend of all the inns of Essex, Spider is immortal,' says James Wentworth Day in his book *In Search of Ghosts* (Frederick Muller, 30s).

The most distinctive thing about Charlie Marshall was his sideways walk, like that of a spider-crab. It earned for him the name that he was known by for all of his adult life. He was a pint-sized character, quick and shrewd and unlovely to look at, who should have figured in some Dickens story, but didn't because Dickens died at about the time that Spider was first learning the art of cadging coppers from unwary coach travellers.

It was an art he learned well, though eventually it brought about his horrific end, as James Wentworth Day goes on to relate. 'At the toss of a hat or the sight of a free pint, Spider would do his famous dare— he would scramble up the chimney of the tap-room fireplace and, covered in soot, shoot down the next chimney into the bar parlour. That is if he felt like completing the manoeuvre. Sometimes he did not.

'Somewhere up in that Stygian blackness where the two chimneys unite there is, presumably, a bacon-loft. And there, sometimes, Spider would sit, full of beer, soot, and somnolence, deaf to all entreaties to come down by either chimney.'

Smoking Him Out

'Sometimes he just wouldn't come down,' Dick Wheston told me. 'So they'd shove a bunch of straw up the chimney. Set fire to it, and smoke him out!

'But one Christmas Eve he got owdacious; full o' beer and wouldn't budge for the straw-smoke. So they rammed a bundle of faggots up the chimney and set fire to 'em. Even that didn't budge him. Fact is he never did come down! Must have suffocated. That's the tale.'

But it is by no means the end of the tale. In fact it is the beginning of a haunting that has gone on ever since.

When builders were called in recently to make alterations to The Bear they attempted to open up the chimney stack that concealed Spider's last resting place. Ten feet up the chimney they found a small chamber, six ft by six, which was perhaps a bacon loft and probably served too as a hide during the Civil War.

But before they had time to investigate it a crack six ft long and wide enough to push one's fist into opened up in the brickwork of the chimney breast, putting the whole place in danger of imminent collapse. So it was decided to leave Spider alone and let him haunt in peace.

James Wentworth Day recalls the comment of landlord Dick Wheston: 'I reckon he's still there. And there he stops. We don't want to lose him. The old chaps often see him dodging about in his boots and white breeches, no higher than a handspan. You see, he's shrunk since he became a ghost. We reckon he's part of the fixings. That's

The Bear Inn, Stock (No. 40)

why the Huntsman, the Master of the Beagles, and a whole host of hunting people turned up to drink his health at Christmas. He's our oldest customer.'

Spider is not the only ghost at The Bear, but he is by far the most entertaining. The others, the footsteps in the night, the suffocating presence that lurks behind locked doors—are more orthodox, more intent on their mundane business of chilling spines. Not so Spider; he's a friend of the family. Almost.

Gloucestershire

Trouble Indeed...

41 TROUBLE HOUSE, Cherington.
A Wadworth house, on the A433 Cirencester to Tetbury road. Open : 10 to 2.30 & 6 to 10.30. Sunday : 12 to 2 & 7 to 10.30. Snacks at bar. Parking. Nearest station : Kemble (6 mls.). It has a railway station of its own, 'Trouble House Halt', but no trains. The line was closed in 1964. Telephone : Tetbury 206.

WHEN THE 18th century was still in its teens this was a dreamy little inn all thatch and roses known as the Waggon and Horses. There had been trouble some fifty years earlier when a party of Royalists quaffing ale and chatting up the landlord's wife were disturbed by some of Cromwell's men on their way to do battle at Worcester.

Fifty years later there was more trouble when the Luddites, after a day on the Waggon, so to speak, were out in force burning and pillaging, causing a near riot that only the army was able to put down.

Worse was to come. The pub fell into decay. The roof sagged, the walls bulged and the landlord of the day had no option but to pull it down. Halfway through the rebuilding he went bankrupt and in a fit of despair hanged himself. The half-finished house was taken over by another but he too ran out of money and drowned himself before he completed it.

So the squire took on the job of rebuilding and when it was finished re-named it the Trouble House to commemorate the two landlords who had died in the attempt.

With a history like that the Trouble House could scarcely fail to have a ghost.

Mr W G Bertwistle, a director of Wadworth, the Wiltshire brewers, first heard about the haunting at the Trouble House in 1936. The tenant in those days was an elderly man who quite often heard the sound of chains being dragged along the stone-floored passage leading to the cellar and at times an inexplicable wind gusting past him.

Mr Bertwistle recalls: 'Several years later I attended a change of tenancy. The story about the chains and the wind was told to the new tenant and his wife, a comparatively young couple. They thought it very amusing, suggesting it was pure imagination. However, just before the last war, during a visit to the Trouble House they told me that their attitude had changed. They related their experiences to explain why.

'On two occasions during the winter evenings, after the customers had gone, the tenant and his wife sat by the fire in the tap room. The oak front door which was heavily barred, suddenly swung open and there was a great gust of wind. The door then closed and the tenant's wife asked her husband why he had not barred the door as usual. He stoutly denied not barring the door. When they both went to investigate, the door was barred as always.'

Outside that door hangs an inn sign that is a potted political history of the pub's troubled past, a reminder of those dramatic events of yesteryear, any one of which may have left its ghostly imprint.

The Mysterious Inscription

42   BLACK HORSE HOTEL, Castle Street, Cirencester.
A Courage house in the town centre. Open : 10 to 2.30 & 6 to 10.30. Serves food. Accommodation : four double rooms. Nearest station : Kemble, Gloucester. Telephone : Cirencester 3094 and 3187.

AT MIDNIGHT on August 13, 1933, a curious thing happened in Cirencester. Mystery writing appeared on the glass of an upstairs window of the Black Horse Hotel. The bedroom was occupied that night by a young woman who reported seeing the ghost of an elderly woman. She described this ghost as 'old-fashioned,' dressed in a fawn coloured dress, white apron and mob cap, and gliding about the room in a flood of soft light.

When the guest screamed the ghost seemed to go through a wall and the aura of light with her.

But in the morning there was the writing—the word 'John' written upside down several times and several capital W's—scratched on the window, as if by a diamond.

A local medium, asked to investigate this phenomenon, said she could 'see' figures, dressed in both white and brown, who were chanting and fingering their beads. Presumably these were the ghosts of monks, who had lived here before the Black Horse first became an inn 400 years ago.

This mellowed building of Cotswold stone with its gabled roof of lichen-crusted sandstone, is the amalgamation of two inns, the Black Horse and the King's Arms, which until World War II traded independently side by side.

Recently, a woman, now over 90 years old, called at the Black Horse and asked to be allowed to look round the house. The landlord gave her a conducted tour, after which she told him that she was the daughter of a previous landlord, one of a family of six born there. She spoke too of another ghost, that she remembered from her life there as a girl— 'A beautiful young woman who appeared dressed in grey. A very happy ghost,' she said.

The Tragic Chambermaid

43 THE OLD BELL, Dursley.
*A Courage house in Long Street. Open: 10 to 2.30 & 6 to 10.30.
Sunday: 12 to 2 & 7 to 10.30. Accommodation. Lunches and dinner.
Own car park. Nearest station: Gloucester. Telephone: Dursley
2821/2033.*

THE VOICE outside the bedroom door said it was 8 o'clock. It was the
voice of a woman, who tried the door handle as she called the time.
Mr Geoffrey McEwan, the visitor from Wallsend-on-Tyne, in Room No. 7
of The Old Bell, thanked her and switched on the light. His watch said
3.30, but as it had been erratic of late he didn't pay much attention to it.
Because he was going to an early appointment he'd asked for a call at
7.30 and assumed this was it, though it was a little late.

'I got up and dressed,' says Mr McEwan. 'It was dark when I opened
the curtains so I thought I'd go downstairs to check the time. Outside
my room everything was deathly quiet. The lights were out in the
passage and no one was stirring. The clock in the restaurant showed
a quarter-past three. The only solution I could think of was that there
had been someone in the passage who had got the wrong room, so
I got back to bed and went straight to sleep. I got my early call promptly
at 7.30 as arranged.'

At breakfast Mr McEwan spoke to the landlady about being knocked
up in the early hours. Only then did he learn something of the history
of this 15th-century inn—that it had once been an assize court
where at least two death sentences were passed, that in 1680 a murder
had been committed in one of the rooms, that a concealed passage
connected his room with Room No. 6, where a young chambermaid
had hanged herself after realising she was pregnant by a soldier who
had run out on her. This last was a tragedy that happened at the turn
of the century and it was her ghost that had called Mr McEwan as it
had done many visitors before him, always at around 3 in the morning.

But Mrs Marie Dykes, a waitress at The Old Bell, has seen the ghost
of the chambermaid in the daytime standing in the doorway to the
dining-room.

'I felt the presence of someone else in the room,' said Mrs Dykes.
'I turned round and there was a girl in the doorway. She had on a long
dress and something dangling down by her side. I don't know what it
was. I think it was a chain. She did not speak. I said, "Can I help you?"
She beckoned to me and made for the stairs, but when I got to the
bottom of the stairs she had disappeared. I know she was a ghost
because of the way she glided along!'

Mrs Dykes added that she did not mind going into Rooms 6 or 7 of
The Old Bell, but Room 9 along the same corridor, 'is haunted as well
and it feels terrible in there.'

In spite of Mrs Dykes's encounter with the ghostly chambermaid and
the experience of Mr McEwan, the landlord does not believe in ghosts.
Yet one afternoon he and his wife witnessed something unusual in the

hotel kitchen. The call bell for Room 6 rang out loud and clear, yet at that time the bells had not been electrically connected to the bell-push in the room . . .

Prisoner at the Bear

44 THE OLDE BLACK BEAR, Tewkesbury.
*A Whitbread/Flowers house in the town centre. Open : 10 to 2.30 &
6 to 10.30. Sunday : 12 to 2 & 7 to 10.30. Snacks. Parking. Nearest
station : Ashchurch (2 mls.). Telephone : Tewkesbury 2202.*

THE OLDEST inn in Gloucestershire, this, and one of the oldest in the whole country. It was built in 1309 though probably an inn stood on this site from the time King John's Bridge was built in 1190. The ghost that haunts the beamed and panelled corridors is a headless man, who appears to be dragging chains as he walks—presumably a prisoner who was beheaded. Perhaps it originated with the Wars of the Roses, since a great number of Lancastrian soldiers defeated at the Battle of Tewkesbury in 1481, fled into the town and took refuge at the Black Bear. So did Turpin from time to time, tethering Black Bess to a tree outside, spurning the landlord's offer, still to be seen on the lounge wall, of stabling for horses at 'Three for a Penny.'

The Patter of Tiny Feet

45 YE OLD CORNER CUPBOARD, Winchcombe.
*A Whitbread/Flowers house in Gloucester Street. Open : 10 to 2 &
6 to 10.30. Sunday : 12 to 2 & 7 to 10.30. Snacks. Parking. Nearest
station : Cheltenham (7½ mls.). Telephone : Winchcombe 0242/
602303.*

BEFORE HENRY VIII decided that the monasteries must go, Winchcombe had a thriving community centred on its Abbey. This little pub was part of it. Its monastic beginnings are evident both outside and in—the four buttresses without, the stonework within. The well discovered below the cellar floor probably provided the monks with water, not only for beer making, but also for bathing the feet of holy men, pilgrims and the like who passed this way, heading ultimately for Glastonbury and the Holy Grail.

   Winchcombe's best-known ghost may well be one of these long-distance travellers who never completed his pilgrimage. This phantom figure is tall and hooded. He glides rather than walks, always about two feet above ground level, along a stretch of road known locally as 'The Monk's Walk.'

It is a part of the Cheltenham road which runs through a hollow near the cemetery where one Winchcombe man had his silent company for 50 nightmarish yards until the figure turned off the road and vanished in the night.

Yet the ghost that haunts Ye Old Corner Cupboard, a building said to be near on 900 years old and, for many of those centuries, a place closely allied with the comings and goings of the monks, does not seem to be one of them. Judging by the patter of tiny feet, it is the ghost of a child, heard often about the house on several occasions by the lunchtime regulars.

'It sounds just like a little girl running overhead, straight through what is now a wall,' says Ron Cousins, the licensee. 'It is not at all frightening. We think it is a charming little ghost but we would like to know more about her.'

Hampshire

The Whimpering Dog

46 CROWN INN, Alton.
*A Courage house in the town centre. Open: 10.30 to 2.30 & 6 to
10.30. Sunday: 12 to 2 & 7 to 10. Lunches only. Nearest station:
Alton. Telephone: Alton 82330 or 84567.*

A WHIMPERING, scratching dog haunts this 15th-century coaching
inn. It is said that the animal died at the hands of its master who in a
drunken rage beat it to death against the chimney-breast in the dining-
room.

Says the landlord: 'I have never seen the ghost, but I have heard
the scratching, and once my two Pekinese dogs went absolutely frantic
when they were near the chimney-breast in that room.'

In 1967 workmen doing alterations at the pub removed a false wall,
behind which, near the original dining-room hearth, they found the
skeleton of a dog.

A Ghost that Rolls the Barrels

47 THE WHITE HART, Basingstoke.
*A Courage house in London Road, ½ mile from the A30. Open:
10 to 2.30 & 6 to 10.30. Sunday: 12 to 2 & 7 to 10. Snacks. Parking.
Nearest staton: Basingstoke. Telephone: Basingstoke 4384.*

THINGS THAT GO bump in the night are common enough. So too is
the stealthy tread of unseen feet. Knockings and rappings in the walls
of buildings saturated in time are heard initially with alarm and later
accepted as just one of those things you live with in an eccentric old
building.

Under the cement rendering and whitewash of Basingstoke's White
Hart is a ghostly sound that is an oddity in pub hauntings. One can
only puzzle at what might be the cause and leave the words of Mrs
Vivian Oliver, wife of a former licensee, to describe it.

'At any time after 12 o'clock midnight, and only after the light was
turned off, this noise used to start. Beginning at the far end of the

room, moving towards the window, it would seem that someone or something was moving on gravel or rolling something along. The sound would roll towards you, till it was just above one's head, say about three feet, then stop and roll back towards the next room. But it never made any noise in that room at all. Then it would start all over again. You either dropped off to sleep or put the light on and then the noise would stop. Sometimes it would be louder than at other times and then one would sleep all night in the chair, with the light on.'

The room which is haunted by this sound was occupied by Mrs Oliver's sister, 'a sensible 40-year-old and not at all over-imaginative.' A similar noise was heard in the small yard at the rear of the inn by one of the staff, who also had the sensation of a presence which he never saw as a definable image. This he noted was at about 5.30 in the morning and happened soon after extensive alterations to the inn had been completed in 1968.

Only once did anybody encounter an apparition during the period from September 1968 to January 1969, when the ghostly sound of rolling barrels was again in evidence at The White Hart.

Mrs Oliver gives this account of what happened in the early morning a few days before Christmas: 'My mother woke feeling cold and a little afraid. She said she lifted her head from the pillow and saw a man, or someone, push open the door and move towards the dressing table. It stopped and with both hands smoothed back its hair, then turned to face the bed, smiled and walked out, leaving the door ajar. She said she called "Viven (that's me), is that you," and, of course, there was no reply.'

The Naked One-Legged Man

48 THE ROYAL OAK, Langstone Village, Havant.
A Brickwoods house on the Havant to Hayling Island road (B2149).
Open: 10 to 2.30 & 6 to 10.30. Serves snacks. Accommodation:
3 double and 15 singles. Parking in street adjacent. Nearest station:
Havant. Telephone: Havant 3125.

'I WAS AGAIN awakened suddenly, by the feeling of a "presence" in my room. Thinking it was my daughter standing by my bed, I asked what she wanted. I got no reply and thought she must be sleep-walking, but as I sat up intending to lead her back to her room, the figure slowly glided away and disappeared through the corner of the room.'

That's how the wife of the landlord describes the haunting at The Royal Oak, a whitewashed pub that has squatted at the edge of a tidal creek in Langstone Harbour for a hundred years or more. The building has been there longer, probably since the middle 16th century, certainly as long as the old mill, a few paces along the shore-path that leads to Warblington Church which has 12th-century beginnings. At one time part of the pub building was a bakery, getting its flour straight from the neighbouring grindstone and supplying fresh bread to Nelson's fleet anchored off Selsey Bill.

None of which in any way relates to the ghostly happenings experienced by Mrs Spring, the landlord's wife, who well remembers, during her first few weeks at The Royal Oak, plainly hearing unaccountable footsteps on the stairs and noises which sounded like chains being moved on the stone floor of the empty public bar.

'In those days we had a spaniel who used to sleep in the bar every night. One night I was awakened by her howling, and, on coming down to find out why, I found her trembling with fear, and bristling all over. She pushed passed me and ran up to my bedroom, and from that day, she would never stay alone in the bar.

'Visitors staying here have heard movements in the next room when no one has been there, and one who booked in for a week last summer, left after one night!'

The Uneasy Silence

One wonders if there is any connection between the ghost at The Royal Oak and the naked one-legged man, encountered by Fred Bason and described by him in these words:*

'I always write of what I see and know. I leave fiction to others. Having said that, I will tell you of a ghost I saw. Take out a map of England: you will see the tiny village of Langstone, near Havant, in Hampshire, opposite Hayling Island. Langstone is at the foot of the tall bridge leading to Hayling Island. Dear friends of mine at the Petersfield Bookshop loaned me after my illness a room above a storage place close to an old windmill that had been converted into living quarters, where I could stay and look after myself and get well in peace and quiet.

'You go up the main street of some twenty tiny houses from the mill, pass over the main road (Havant–Hayling motor-bus road); facing you then is a quiet shady lane leading to wide marshes and smooth mud (little sand) for miles. At ten one morning I went down this lane on my way to catch the bus to Portsmouth. It was a bright day and the birds were singing. I was happy. Then suddenly it seemed as if all was silent. I stopped. I felt uneasy. In front of me, not more than twenty feet away, there lay on the ground a naked man, and he had half a right leg—a stump above the knee. He was old—I would say well past sixty—and bald and awfully thin. I walked forward slowly, and I was afraid. There was silence in that lane. I looked around, thinking I should need help; there was no one about at all. I walked nearer and was within three or at the most four yards—the distance of an ordinary room—when the man vanished. He didn't fade away, he simply vanished. But I saw that man with my own two eyes on the ground stark naked—and I say that I saw a ghost.'

* In the ninth edition of The Saturday Book, edited by Leonard Russell (Hutchinson).

'Now comes a sequel,' wrote Mr Bason in *The Saturday Book* of the following year: 'Early this year I had a visit from Mr Edward Greer, a former civil servant, who lives near Havant, in Hampshire. He was in London and thought he'd pop over to look me up, buy a few books, and confirm my own and only experience of seeing a ghost—*for he had seen the same figure in the same lane five years before I had!* He described the quiet shady lane that leads on to swampy land where you have to be very careful or you will sink down pretty deep in a few seconds. He described the body, mentioning the grey matted hair on the chest which I had seen but had left out of my short narrative. Mr Greer agreed with me on the extreme thinness of the body, but whereas I had said the head was bald, he recalled a fringe of grey hair rather bushy at the back. I closed my eyes and visualised again the figure lying there, but could not recall a fringe of hair—I could still see the bald head. But it is reasonable to suggest that we might not have seen the figure at the same angle.

'I asked Mr Greer if he'd made any inquiries locally about a one-legged man, and he said that he had. The ghostly figure had shocked him as it had shocked me. But whereas I had gone on down the lane, he had retraced his footsteps, crossed the main road, gone down the tiny main street of Langstone, and into the local for a pint to "steady himself." Over his pint he related his experience to a couple of locals in the bar. He fully described to them the naked one-legged man, very thin and rather long in the body, and he was even able to describe his thin long nose, which he called the Duke of Wellington kind. Neither of the men was able to recall a one-legged man in those parts, when in came a third party, another local. When the question was put to the newcomer he thought for a moment—oh, yes, he did remember a one-legged man, very thin, very tall. He walked with a crutch and carried a haversack in which there were not combs or shoelaces but miniature Bibles and hundreds of little text-cards in colour.

The Aristocratic Nose

'The man was an evangelist, and it was his habit to stop passers-by and ask, "Have you been saved?" And then he'd hand them a text or two or some Bible readings in pamphlet form. He never asked for money; don't know how he got his living. Never heard of anybody buying a little Bible off him. The man had come several times to Langstone, perhaps as late as 1932 or 1933—then no more. Mr Greer asked what sort of a face the evangelist had, but his informant couldn't remember anything except that he had *one of those aristocratic noses, thin and high in the middle!*

'Mr Greer stood the three men a pint each. He was quite satisfied that the preacher fellow had come to harm in that thickly treed lane, or on the marshlands, and that he'd seen his ghost. Then he forgot the incident until he read Volume 9 of *The Saturday Book* and discovered that I had seen the same ghostly figure. I saw the ghost in September of 1945. Edward Greer saw it in June or July of 1940.'

The Royal Oak, Langstone Village (No. 48)

The Forsaken Wife

49 KIMPTON DOWN INN, Kimpton.
A Strongs house 9 miles north of the A303 at Thruxton. Open:
10 to 2.30 & 6 to 10.30 (Saturday to 11). Sunday: 12 to 2.30 & 7 to 11.
Nearest station: Andover Junction. Telephone: WEY 444.

UNTIL THE mid-sixties this was just another village pub, squatting on the very edge of the vast expanse of Salisbury Plain. Then quite suddenly things began to happen—at about the time the builders moved in to make alterations to the black-beamed, low-ceilinged lounge bar.

This structural disturbance apparently resulted in a considerable amount of poltergeist-like activity—ornaments were swept from the mantlepiece by an unseen hand, bottles of beer were swept from a shelf and smashed on the bar counter, plates of food were turned upside-down. Then the licensee's wife and daughter and a number of customers reported seeing 'the faint outline of a figure'—usually during the afternoon or evening. A drayman of Strongs, the Romsey brewers, refused to deliver to the pub on account of these happenings both the area manager and the surveyor said that visiting the premises made them feel uneasy. In the village there are folk who believe the ghost is that of a former landlord's wife who was left to die in the locked cellar of the inn.

The Fugitive Highwayman

50 ROYAL ANCHOR HOTEL, Liphook.
A three star Courage house, on the A3 to Portsmouth. 'Its hours of opening,' says the landlord, 'are from 7.30 a.m. until the last guest arrives.' Serves lunch and dinner. Accommodation: 21 bedrooms. Parking for 50 cars. Nearest station: Liphook. Telephone: Liphook 2244.

EDWARD II knew little about kingship but plenty about hunting. A day chasing the buck in the Royal Hampshire Forests of Woolmer was much to be preferred to a day of arguing the toss with a castleful of quarrelsome barons.

In those days Woolmer enclosed the hamlet of Liphook on two sides and at Liphook there was a cosy little three-star place with a plentiful supply of liquor where the royal presence could enjoy the frivolities of life without interruption. And to be sure that indigestion didn't curb his pleasures between the sheets he took his own cook.

Two and a half centuries later when Queen Elizabeth stopped there on her way to Cowdray Castle to visit the Montagues, Edward's hunting lodge had become the bustling Blue Anchor, with four-posters in all bedrooms.

The Royal Anchor Hotel, Liphook (No. 50)

James I enjoyed the hospitality of the Anchor. So did Charles II. Samuel Pepys was there on the night of August 6, 1668 and noted in his diary: . . . 'So to coach again, and got to Liphook; late over Hindhead, having an old man, a guide, in the coach with us; but got thither with great fear of being out of our way, it being ten at night. Here good honest people; and after supper to bed.'

Then came Queen Anne who, in between producing nineteen offspring, made a number of sorties to Liphook to follow the stag hunt in an open one-horse chaise, which, said Dean Swift, 'she drives herself and drives like Jehu.' After her there was George III who came with his Queen and dubbed the inn the Royal Anchor. When William IV stayed he would sit in the kitchen which he said was 'the merriest room in the house,' and eat bread and cheese with a clasp knife.

Nelson stopped there and the Queens of Spain and Portugal. So did John Wilkes, the Duke of Wellington and Marshal Blücher, and, of course, Victoria and her Albert. Yet not one of that spectacular collection of celebrities left behind a ghost to walk the ancient boards of the Anchor, to haunt its maze of tunnels and secret rooms.

That honour goes to a highwayman, a Captain Jacques who did his foulest deeds and earned his lushest pickings on the ten miles of road that dips and rears between Liphook and Petersfield. Until the coming of the railway in 1859 the road to Portsmouth was one of the busiest in the country. As many as 24 coaches a day changed horses at the Anchor before running the gauntlet of desperadoes like Captain Jacques.

The Concealed Door

His activities came to a sudden end, when cornered by the Excise men in Room No. 6 at the Anchor Hotel. He was shot down trying frantically to open a concealed door, behind the big fireplace. From there a narrow secret staircase led down to the floor below and then down to the cellar. He, better than anyone, knew the warren of tunnels leading in all directions from the hotel cellar. There was one in particular leading under the Square for about 100 yards which would have allowed him to escape through the packed bar of the old Ship Inn, which is now Lloyds Bank.

Roger Newman, a writer and historian who lives in Liphook, told me of his conversation with the widow of a former landlord of the Anchor.

'She told me that an Australian lady came to stay at the Anchor, and was given Room 6. The following morning when she came down to breakfast she asked the landlord if there was a ghost in the building. Apparently three times during the night "a man in a long coat and three-cornered hat"—traditional highwayman apparel—"came out of the fireplace and walked through the door of the bedroom." The third time she followed him, but he vanished in the passage at the top of the stairs.'

An old public house with another ghost in the vicinity was The Plough, at Redford (on the Liphook to Midhurst road, and i. West

Sussex). Unfortunately the pub was demolished in 1970. The ghost was that of a tall lady who had the disturbing habit of standing behind non-regular customers, smiling and then vanishing. The pub was empty for some four years before it was pulled down.

The Shadowy Coachman
and the Spectral Piano

1   THE ANGEL, Lymington.
An Eldridge Pope house in the High Street. Open: 10 to 2.30 &
6 to 10.30. Sunday: 12 to 2 & 7 to 10.30. Accommodation: 24 bed-
rooms. Lunch and dinner. Parking. Nearest station: Lymington.
Telephone: Lymington 2050.

MEN WHO CUT the New Forest oaks and others who fashioned them into the ships of Henry VIII's navy, used this house, but called it by a different name. To them it was The George, after the patron saint of England. It was the local of the Lymington ship builders and of the men who sailed in the vessels they built.

It was not until 1756, when a George was on the throne, that it is first referred to in the Borough records as The Angel, by which time it was less a tavern and more a hostelry, catering for the rapidly growing number of people who were encouraged to travel in 'the fast and fashionable stagecoach.'

In 1768 the cost of travelling by coach was a shilling for five miles and, with frequent changes of horse, coaches could cover between 50 and 100 miles a day with ease—if the passengers could stand the strain. At the turn of the 18th century London was only two days' fast drive from The Angel's front door while the cathedral cities of Salisbury and Winchester, with their bustling markets were only a few hours away.

In later years it was one of the sights of Lymington to watch the departure of the Royal Mail coach, which left The Angel at 4.45 pm daily and rattled and swayed its way over the rutted New Forest roads to Southampton and on to London.

When, in 1782, one of the best known of the Regency illustrators, Thomas Rowlandson, travelled to Portsmouth to view the wreck of the *Royal George*, he put up at The Angel, which had then become one of the most delightful coaching inns in the south of England.

With so much of its history bound up with the coaching age, it is little wonder that at least one of the ghosts that haunt The Angel is the shadowy figure of a coachman, seen in the dawn light standing by the kitchen window, staring out into the yard.

There is also a ghost that stems from the inn's close association with the sea—a tall grey-haired figure, wearing a naval-style coat with brass buttons fastening to the neck.

'He appeared momentarily to me about 11.30 pm on one occasion,'

The Angel, Lymington (No. 51)

says Mr John Dicker, who was a relief manager at The Angel. 'I was at the hotel only for a fortnight, but I understood that this ghost has been seen by others.'

A more unusual paranormal experience was reported by Mr M E McKinley, who was manager at The Angel for five years until 1968. In a letter Mr McKinley says: 'It is worth recalling the experience of my brother's wife when they stayed with us some two years ago. They were given the bedroom adjoining the old assembly hall which had its heyday 100 years ago, as the framed announcement of a "grand ball" dated 1860 testifies.

'On the first night my sister-in-law retired to bed early while my brother and I remained in the bar until midnight. After locking up the hotel I went along to say a final goodnight to my sister-in-law. She was sitting up in bed, wide-eyed with amazement that I should allow anyone to thump on the piano keys at such an unearthly hour. She was not to know that the piano, long beyond repair, had been removed the day before and broken up. Her experience was apparently real, for she remained unconvinced by my explanation and insisted that my brother and I should unlock the hall and make a thorough search. We did so—and found nothing.'

The Battered Brushmaker

52 BRUSHMAKERS' ARMS, Shoe Lane, Upham.
A Watney house, just off the Bishop Waltham to Winchester road (A333). Open: 10 to 2 & 6 to 10.30. Nearest station: Winchester. Telephone: Durley 231.

WHILE OLIVER CROMWELL was making ready to attack Winchester he put up at this inn. There is a tiny alcove, now used as a smoking room, where the man who was to become the one and only dictator of all England, thumbed his maps and laid his plans for the Roundhead advance. The ivy-clad church across the road provided stabling for the Roundhead cavalry, which didn't endear them to the villagers.

A hundred years before Cromwell did battle in these parts this pub was thriving, catering for the colony of brushmakers who congregated in the vale of Upham when they were not tramping the countryside selling their new brooms of hazel sticks cut from the green hedgerows of Hampshire.

One of these was a man named Chickett, a miser. He probably made more money out of the brushmaking business than anybody else in Upham. He'd been in the trade a long time. The brooms he made were that bit better than the next man's and Miser Chickett knew how to sell them at better prices. Today he'd be an ace vacuum cleaner salesman, paying a fat monthly cheque into a healthy bank account. As it was, he hoarded every penny he made and took it with him everywhere he went.

At night he slept with it under the bed in a low-ceilinged, not unpleasant little room at the front of the inn.

There too he died, his battered body left sprawled on a blood-soaked bed, his savings gone except for a gold piece or two which fell as his murderers fled.

Chickett's murderers were never found, but Chickett's ghost has put in many an appearance since the day the old miser was done to death. At least it is thought to be Chickett's ghost that prowls the same low-ceilinged little room at the front of the Brushmakers' Arms, though there is a belief that the place is haunted by the ghost of a former landlord, murdered while counting the day's takings.

Whatever the ghost there are some among the local folk who would not care to spend the night in what was Miser Chickett's bedroom, and one landlord had a dog that showed a strange restlessness on occasions. As if aware of some unseen, ominous presence it would lay back its ears and growl menacingly.

Not only to the seeker after haunted inns is the Brushmakers' Arms a fascinating pub; it is a picturesque place with a slice of history all its own. It still has a skittle alley where the young blades once spent their time between cock-fights and courting, courting perhaps at the end of the garden, near the well. But not too near, since the well is 175 feet deep. If you drop a penny in you can count up to seven before you hear the low rumble as the coin splashes into the water. That allows plenty of time for wishing.

The Restless Spirit of Dame Alice

53 THE ECLIPSE, The Square, Winchester.
A Strong house, in the shadow of the Cathedral. Open : 10 to 2.30 & 6 to 10.30. Friday & Saturday to 11. Accommodation : 2 doubles, 1 single. Serves food. Parking adjacent. Nearest station : Winchester. Telephone : Winchester 5676.

ON SEPTEMBER 2, 1685, Dame Alice Lisle stepped from an upper window of the Eclipse inn in Winchester's market place, laid her head on the block and was beheaded.

She went to her death in the shadow of the ancient cathedral, with the calm dignity of an old lady, having been sentenced at the Bloody Assizes by the foul-mouthed Judge Jeffreys. She paid the extreme penalty for hiding two men from Monmouth's rebellion.

If the notorious judge had had his way she would have been dragged through the streets of Winchester on a hurdle and burned alive. But the king, fearful of the men of Hampshire and heeding the words of warning from the Bishop of Winchester, reprieved her from this horrible end.

So a scaffold was built, hard against the timbered front wall of the Eclipse inn and Dame Lisle spent her last night in a room looking out on the cobbled square, kept from sleep by the banging and cursing of the carpenters.

After the axe had fallen the body was taken to Ellingham, not furtively but triumphantly, hundreds of ordinary Hampshire men and women accompanying this brave old woman to her last resting-place.

Her ghost has not rested. It haunts the Eclipse by dark and by day-light, at times in the bedroom in which Dame Alice spent her last hours. More often it is seen in one of the upstairs passages, usually in the same place. One eye-witness said: 'I was cleaning the carpet on the first floor landing at about 10 in the morning and had a feeling some-body was watching me. I looked over my shoulder and saw a tall woman in a long grey woollen dress standing in a corner of the landing. I could not see her face, just the figure. It was an odd experience which left me rather shaken. The second time was at about 11 in the morning when, in the same passageway I felt someone brush against me, giving me a gentle push. I called out but nobody was there. Although it was uncanny I didn't feel at all frightened.'

The Ghost that Comes in from the Cold

54 HYDE TAVERN, Winchester.
A Marston's house, in Hyde Street, a short walk from the city centre. Open: 12 to 2 & 6 to 10.30. Sunday: 12 to 2 & 7 to 10.30. Snacks at the bar. Street parking only. Nearest station: Winchester. Telephone: Winchester 6061.

THERE ARE FOLK in Winchester who will tell you this is the city's oldest inn. Alfred, they say, was King when this tavern first offered ale and shelter to the travellers of Saxon England. It was part of a Benedictine monastery which Alfred and his son Edward the Elder founded originally in the centre of the city and called Newminster to distinguish it from the old cathedral. More than two centuries later it was renamed Hyde Abbey, when Henry I moved the monastery to the site close to where the tavern stands today. Just around the corner is the old Abbey gateway and across the road is Hyde Church, wherein, say some, King Alfred was buried, not in the Cathedral, as is generally supposed.

When you drink in either of the tavern's low-beamed bars you may well encounter someone who will not only give you the low-down on Winchester's history but also tell you about the ghost that is said to haunt the Tavern. I was told the story by Mrs Dorothy Bowles, a friend of Mr and Mrs David Rice, who were running the Hyde in the mid-sixties and accepted the haunting as something that went with a pub as ancient as this one.

There were times when they woke in the early hours to feel the blankets being slowly pulled from the bed. At other times they would wake in the morning cold and shivering with the bedclothes in a heap on the floor.

'When I slept there,' said Mrs Bowles, 'I occupied the little spare bedroom and sure enough I woke about 4 am, feeling terribly cold and my top blanket on the floor. The second night Mrs Rice felt the blanket being pulled away. She sat up in bed and threw the blanket into the middle of the room, calling out "Take it if you are cold but please leave me alone."

'Everyone says: "Of course the blankets slide off the beds. Look at the angle of the floors, the beds are on a slope." But that is not so. The beds are built-up with blocks to a level position and extra care is taken to see that the blankets are really well tucked in, hospital-style.'

Who then is this ghost who seemingly covets the blankets from other people's beds? Says Mrs Bowles, 'It is thought to be the ghost of a woman who, centuries ago, when the place was used by pilgrims, sought shelter here but was refused and died cold and hungry.'

Herefordshire

A Lost Love?

5 THE FALCON HOTEL, Bromyard.
*A free house in Broad Street. Open: 10.30 to 2.30 & 6 to 10.30.
Sunday: 12 to 2 & 7 to 10.30. Lunches and dinners. Serves snacks
also. Accommodation: 11 bedrooms. Parking (with garage
facilities). Nearest station: Worcester (13½ mls.). Telephone:
Bromyard 2108.*

AN ANCIENT inn this, though much modernised in recent years—
but this without sacrificing the splendid panelling or the forest of ageing
beams. Its ghost does not seem to be of the same 1620 vintage as the
inn itself. A double sighting reported in the Press in 1964 described
it as the ghost of a young man which appeared on the second floor,
and said: 'Where is Ann?'

Hertfordshire

The Big Fat Man

56 OLDE KING'S ARMS, High Street, Hemel Hempstead.
*A McMullens (of Hertford) pub in the old town centre. Open:
10 to 2.30 & 6 to 10.30. Friday and Saturday: 6 to 11. Specialises in
Chinese cooking. Parking. Nearest station: Hemel Hempstead.
Telephone: Hemel Hempstead 55348.*

HERE'S A PUB that is not only said to have links with Henry VIII
during the time he was courting Anne Boleyn, but also sports the coat
of arms of Edward VI, his son by Queen Jane. It has oak beams, both
inside and out, enough to build a Tudor battleship. The dining-room
has an impressive inglenook fireplace, overlooked by a minstrels'
gallery. And there is a galleried courtyard, a pleasant reminder of
stagecoach travel.

A whipcrack away from all this old world architecture is the swinging
new town of Hemel Hempstead and the M1, but their nearness doesn't
stop the ghosts from walking. Every now and then a lady-in-white
appears . . .

The Olde King's Arms specialises in Cantonese cooking and two
Chinese chefs who have occupied the same room independently of
each other, have both reported seeing 'a big fat man who come and
sit by bed and laugh.'

It is worth recalling that Henry VIII stood six feet four inches and his
girth increased so much in later years that he had to have armour
specially made for him. Even without armour he had to be swung on
to his horse by a pulley, but that was no laughing matter.

Juliet of Holywell

57 FERRY BOAT INN, Holywell, St Ives.
*A free house 2 miles east of St Ives off A1123, the Earith to Hunting-
don road. Open : 11 to 2.30 & 6 to 10.30. Sunday : 12 to 2 & 7 to 10.30.
Lunch and dinner. Accommodation. Parking. Nearest station :
St Ives (or to Huntingdon & then bus). Telephone : St Ives 63227.*

TOM ZOUL, with the good looks and the broad, bronzed shoulders,
was a woodcutter. Had his wit been as sharp as his axe he would have
been the heart-throb of the fenlands.

As it was he lived only for his job and spent most evenings supping
ale in the parlour of the ferryman's cottage, which in those days, before
the Battle of Hastings, was as good a place as any for a beer and a
gossip.

The woods Tom worked by day flanked the cottage on three sides.
On the fourth the brown, reed-filled waters of the Great Ouse flowed
sluggishly past the front door-step, making it the safest place to step
ashore from the ferryboat and doubly convenient for travellers who had
developed a thirst coming across the marshes.

This was Hereward-the-Wake country. He knew these marshes like the
wrinkles on his old mother's face, and crossed the river at this very
spot when fleeing from the rampaging Normans.

And it was here that Juliet Tousley, a delicate and lovely 19-year-old
from the village, used to come and sit under the willows at the water's
edge waiting for Tom to finish his work so that she could walk home
with him.

She was desperately in love with Tom and hurt by his persistant
indifference. Until a bleak day in the March of 1050, when she decided
she could endure it no more. They met but only to quarrel and, in the
mist shrouded dawn of March 18, Tom, walking to work, found her body
hanging from a willow, the one she had so often sat under while waiting
for him.

He cut her down and helped to bury her. She was still dressed in
her best pink gown when the mourning villagers laid her in a watery
grave, a few paces from the river-bank, hard by the cottage where Tom
did his drinking. Over her they laid a stone, a plain slab of rough-hewn
granite.

The Ferry Boat Inn, St Ives (No. 57)

As Holywell grew the ferryman's cottage became the Ferry Boat Inn. Permission was given to succeeding landlords to add other rooms, even to build over Juliet's unconsecrated grave, using the stone slab as part of the floor.

Today, the stone, marking Juliet's grave, is still there, trodden smooth by nine centuries of customers. It is noticeable because it is a little larger and a little higher than the other stones surrounding it. On one night of the year, St Patrick's night, at midnight, it is more noticeable still, when the ghost of Juliet materialises above it.

As described in my book *The Ghost Tour* (Wolfe Publishing): 'On the night of March 17th, the Ferry Boat is packed almost to its neat thatched roof with people watching and waiting for Juliet's ghost to materialise through the bar floor and to drift out to the waiting Ouse. Sometimes the landlord gets a late extension for Juliet's night out and then extra police from near-by St Ives (where Oliver Cromwell lived) are detailed to control the crowd which includes ghosthunters from all over the world—and a generous sprinkling of merrymaking students from Cambridge, thirteen miles down the road.'

The bar of the Ferry Boat Inn

The New Inn, St Neots (No. 59)

The Shade of Cromwell

58 THE GOLDEN LION, St Ives.
A Patons, Bass Charrington hotel in the Market Place. Open: 10.30 to 2.30 (Monday to 4.30) & 6 to 10.30. Friday & Saturday to 11. Sunday: 12 to 2 & 7 to 10.30. Snacks, lunch and dinner. Accommodation. Parking. Nearest station: Huntingdon (6 mls.). Telephone: St Ives 3159.

SINCE OLIVER CROMWELL was so closely associated with this part of England, it's the most likely place for his ghost to make an appearance. Hereabouts he was born, here he farmed and here he trained the volunteers—Puritan freeholders and farmers of the Eastern counties —who formed the spearhead of the Ironside army. 'Cromwell's Barn' which was his drill hall, still exists, and in the Golden Lion Hotel there is a room thought to have been used by Cromwell and his top brass as their district headquarters. A private stairway which led to this room from the courtyard of The Golden Lion ensured that the Roundheads could enter the building without being seen from the public rooms.

Cromwell's room, now a bedroom furnished in the style of the Cromwellian period, was No. 13, but superstitious visitors declined to sleep in the room after reports of 'strange noises in the night.' Changing the room number to 12 didn't stop what is thought to be Cromwell's ghost from appearing, as one woman guest discovered. She saw a shadowy shape of a man dressed in Cromwellian clothes walk into the bedroom in the early hours of the morning.

It is widely believed in St Ives that the Lord Protector's ghost walks on the night of the 13th day of each month along a particular upstairs corridor of The Golden Lion.

That is not the only part of this hotel that has been touched by history. Somewhere at cellar level there is a passage leading to a quayside on the Great Ouse, 70 yards away.

'Old-timers in St Ives swear that their grandfathers used to spin yarns about the strange boat which was seen to tie up at the quayside twice each month with unfailing regularity,' says George Laing, a writer in the *Peterborough Citizen.*

'The story goes,' elaborates Mr Laing, 'that the small boat made its way up the river from the Wash carrying contraband spirits. Stops were made at riverside inns and coaching houses on the way, and spirits were off-loaded. The last port of call was St Ives and there barrels of French brandy, rum and wines were rolled up the cobblestoned tunnel and into the cellars of The Golden Lion.'

So far no one has discovered the underground passage.

The Earl's Return

9 **THE NEW INN, St Neots.**
A Greene King house in town centre. Open: 10.30 to 2.30 & 6 to 10.30. Sunday: 12 to 2 & 7 to 10.30. Lunches and dinner. Accommodation: bed and breakfast. Parking. Nearest station: St Neots. Telephone: Huntingdon 72745.

THE EARL OF HOLLAND lost his head in the Tower of London after being held prisoner in this inn. A number of his officers, taken prisoner at the same time, were executed later in the vicinity of the inn itself. But it is the Earl's ghost that has been seen here, identified from old prints. An eye-witness of the haunting describes him as 'a tall, slender man with an aloof appearance and dressed in an ankle-length cloak.'

Kent

The Body in the Well

60 THE WALNUT TREE, Aldington.
A Shepherd Neame house on B2069 two miles south of the A20 at Smeeth. Snacks and lunches. Dinner to order. Open : 10.30 to 2.30 & 6 to 10.30. Sunday : 12 to 2.30 & 7 to 10.30. Nearest station : Ashford. Telephone : Aldington 298.

GEORGE RANSLEY, who, with his two sons, led the Aldington gang on smuggling missions that could be matched only in daring and effrontery by the infamous Hawkhurst gang, used this pub as his headquarters.

In the early 1800's there was an uninterrupted view across the Romney Marsh from a small window at the back of the inn, from where the gang's shore party could watch for the light that signalled the arrival of the contraband. Once they saw the beam flashing on the coast some five miles away, they would hang a lantern in the window as a homing beacon for 'the gentlemen' and their pad-nags. It was then only matter of time—and patience.

In an upstairs room of The Walnut Tree, the gang used to pass the long hours of waiting in gambling and drinking, often quarrelling. One quarrel more violent than usual ended with a cut throat and a corpse to dispose of. The body supposedly went down the well, since the ghost—perhaps his, perhaps that of his killer—is heard in the early hours of the morning, going to the well, which is still there but unused, at the side of the pub.

Legend has it that there are two ghosts. Maybe this is so, for it takes two at least to make a quarrel. Or is the shade of George Ransley, the instigator of all these crimes, for which he was deported after being cornered in a barn at near-by Bank Farm, back in his old haunt?

The Gentleman in Green Velvet

61 THE CHEQUERS, Bickley.
*A Whitbread house in Southborough Lane. Open: 10.30 to 2.30 &
6.30 to 10.30. Sunday: 12 to 2 & 7 to 10. Snacks and meals. Limited
parking. Nearest station: Bickley. Telephone: 467/3794.*

THAT FELLOW Dick Turpin certainly got around. He can't claim the
record for the most pub beds slept in. Mr Dickens and Mr Pepys are
joint holders of that distinction.

More often than not Dick Turpin didn't have the time to get into bed.
A night in the hayloft was luxury for him. Even when he did get under
the bedcovers he was afraid to take his boots off. He was supposed to
be a regular at The Chequers at Bickley, using the back stairs to make
his escape to a bedroom in the oldest part of the pub in which there was
an enormous four-poster bed with a canopy, hung with long green
curtains, in the folds of which he used to hide.

His ghost is still about. Florrie Tuite, for 19 years a barmaid at The
Chequers, working for three different landlords, thinks 'the gentleman
in green velvet could be Turpin's ghost.'

A few years ago a woman customer looked into an upstairs room in
the older part of this pub with its 16th-century beginnings and was
greeted by a man who sat writing at a table. Which is nothing remarkable
except that the man wrote with an old-fashioned quill pen, was dressed
in green velvet and wore a plumed hat.

The customer who had this strange encounter knew nothing of
Florrie Tuite's theory about Turpin's ghost. She fled downstairs to
complain that a barman in fancy dress had given her the fright of her
life.

There are regulars who talk of other hauntings, of women in 18th-
century clothes seen wandering the upper floors of The Chequers.
After 11 years as landlord, Albert Gordon has become accustomed to
the apparitions, the footsteps in the night, the slamming doors. He has
become accustomed also to waking at night to find the bed shaking.

He says of the customer who saw 'the gentleman in green velvet':
'She is very psychic, and not the type to imagine things. In fact, she is
a very stable woman. There is just no explanation to her experience.'

Mr Gordon says he has often heard footsteps in the rooms above
and thought a burglar was upstairs. A detailed search of the pub has
always proved otherwise. He recalls the time when an inner door was
heard to open and slam shut, followed by footsteps running up the
stairs. When he checked the door he found it bolted. 'When I go on
holiday,' says Mr Gordon, 'friends stay here to help run the pub, and
they have noticed the same things, the same sounds. The wife is Irish
and she says she has spent many sleepless nights because of the
shaking bed and ghostly noises. These strange things seem only to
affect some people. I suppose some of us are psychic and others are
not. I think there is something peculiar in this place. If there is such a
thing as a ghost, I think there is one here.'

The Reverend Gentleman of Chilham

62 WHITE HORSE, Chilham, near Canterbury.
A Whitbread house in the village square, opposite Chilham castle gates. Open: 10 to 2.30 & 6 to 10.30. Sunday: 12 to 2 & 7 to 10.30. Snacks and cold buffet. No accommodation. Parking in the square. Nearest station: Chilham. Telephone: Chilham 355.

IF YOU ARE here just after ten in the morning and see a benign old gentleman seemingly warming himself in front of the 15th-century inglenook fire, you've seen the ghost of this picturesque pub.

In the village—'one of the twelve loveliest villages in England,' to quote from a tourist board handout—it is accepted that this is the ghost of the Rev. Sampson Hieron, a 17th-century vicar of Chilham.

Long before the White Horse became one of the most delightful pubs in Kent, it was Vicar Hieron's home, which is why the grey-haired old man's ghost, black gowned and gaitered, stands with hands behind his back and looking as if he owns the place.

At times he sits, but it is always at the same hour—10 minutes past 10 in the morning—and the moment an unsuspecting customer acknowledges him with a polite 'good morning,' he vanishes, presumably up the massive chimney.

Though the reverend gentleman was evicted from his living for being a nonconformist, he was buried along the road in St Mary's Churchyard when he died in 1677. But before you go to search among the old tombstones have another look at that inglenook in the saloon bar. It dates back to 1460. The Tudor rose carved at each end of the great oak beam supporting the chimney breast is a guarantee of its age. For two centuries it was hidden, preserved in fact, under plaster and brick. Then in 1956 during renovations it was revealed along with the ceiling beams and the moulded timber joists.

Digging under the back kitchen floor of the inn brought to light two complete and perfectly preserved male skeletons. At neighbouring Chilham Castle, diggings in the dungeons unearthed six skeletons, one chained to the wall. A coroner's court pronounced them 'ancient bones' and they were given a Christian burial.

But there are those who still speculate about them over a frothing pint. The general supposition is that they were either men who fell at Chilham during the Wat Tyler rebellion or perhaps even pre-Christian era remains.

Footsteps in the Night

53   BLACK BULL, Church Street, Cliffe, near Rochester.
A Courage pub. Open: 10 to 2.30 & 6 to 11. Snacks at bar. Parking.
No accommodation. Nearest station: Higham. Telephone: Cliffe
278.

THIS IS Dickens country. He got to know it when, as a boy, he was brought here by his father, and later when he was rich and famous. He then lived a few miles along the road at Gadshill. In those days Cliffe Marshes were littered with the hulks of prison ships and populated by grazing sheep. The only habitation was an occasional farm or an isolated weatherboarded cottage.

There are a few people living in Cliffe who can remember when the Black Bull was little more than a cottage of weatherboarding built on the site of an old church. After World War I it was pulled down and rebuilt in the mellow red brick so familiar to the Kentish landscape. That, say some, is why it is haunted. The footsteps heard at night shuffling across the upstairs rooms and the securely fastened door that opens of its own accord are attributed to the suggestion that the Black Bull may have been rebuilt on the old graveyard and not on the site of the old church.

It's an interesting theory and it reminds one that, in the churchyard at neighbouring Cooling a mile along the road, there is a row of ten child-sized gravestones, the resting place of an entire 18th-century family on which Dickens based Pip's family in *Great Expectations*.

Strange Bedfellow

54   SHIPWRIGHT'S ARMS, Hollow Shore, Faversham.
A free house. Open: 10.30 to 3 & 6 to 11. Sundays: 12 to 2 & 7 to
10.30. Sandwiches. Nearest station: Faversham. Telephone:
Faversham 3163.

THE WIND SIGHS in a melancholy voice through the waist-high reeds that thrust up from the acres of polluted mud and marsh that surround this 300-year-old weatherboarded cottage. When the tide is up and the creek is full the Shipwright's Arms is below sea level and one feels more secure in the knowledge that there is a boatyard next door. The *phut-phut-phut* of the little engine that drives the electric lighting plant is equally as reassuring, especially on a thick winter's night when the ghostly foghorns are sounding out in the estuary.

This is a one-bar pub, with nautical trimmings and a nautical ghost— that of an old sea captain, with glaring eyes, thick-set in build and usually wearing a reefer jacket—the kind Victorian seamen often wore. Speculation is that after his ship sank he dragged himself across the mud flats only to die of exposure on the pub's doorstep.

The Shipwright's Arms, Faversham (No. 64)

'I suppose,' says Mr Allen, the licensee, 'that when the door saw opened in the morning his soul came in looking for warmth and comfort. I have never seen him or been troubled by him, but in the winter when the rooms downstairs become cold, doors leading to the warmer rooms are often found open.'

But although Mr Allen has not seen the captain's ghost, the wife of a former licensee has done so—three times.

'I saw this figure standing at the bottom of the bed just looking at me,' she said. 'I experienced the same thing on three consecutive nights. I have also seen the man sitting in the small room adjoining the bar.'

Whenever he appears a strong unfamiliar smell accompanies him, and sometimes a draught of cold air.

A boatbuilder from the yard adjoining the pub was drinking alone in the bar one night. He felt a cold draught and at the same time heard the bar door close. A bearded man in a black tailed coat came in and disappeared. Another night, sleeping at the boatyard, he was shaken awake by an unseen hand.

But the strangest tale of all about this haunting is told by Barry Tester, son of a former licensee, who left the Shipwright's Arms six months before his parents, after waking one exceptionally cold night to find that the ghost had got into bed with him.

NAME-NOTE: *It is just possible that on this spot a few thousand years ago a holy man had his oratory, so giving the place the name of Holy Shore, which is not a long way removed phonetically from Hollow Shore.*

The Phantom with a Whitewash Brush

65   THE KING'S HEAD, Five Oak Green.
A Courage house on B2017 between Paddock Wood and Tudeley. Open : 10 to 2.30 & 6 to 10.30. Sunday : 12 to 2 & 7 to 10. Snacks. Accommodation : 4 bedrooms. Parking. Nearest station : Paddock Wood. Telephone : Paddock Wood 2070.

A REGULAR at the King's Head who for some years lodged at the pub has good cause to remember the ghost with the whitewash brush. He had been redecorating one of the upstairs rooms, spending most of a day chipping old whitewash off one of the ceiling beams in readiness for staining. When he finished in the evening he left his paint and brushes in the room, ready for an early start in the morning. That's where the ghost took a hand. By morning the beam was finished, repainted with whitewash!

There are other ways in which this ghost shows its liking for decoration; it steals lipsticks and earrings. 'But,' says Mrs Stan Hardstone, the landlady of The King's Head, 'it's not a malicious ghost; it does sometimes take things that are treasured by someone. Oddly, it has its

busy weeks and its slack ones. We'll hear nothing of it for two or three weeks and then it does several things in a few days.

'It moves about at night and locks doors on the inside while people are sleeping. It does not restrict itself to any one room and has twice been seen moving across the saloon bar, just as a dark shape, once at 3 pm and once at 12.45 am.'

A previous landlady described the ghost as 'an elderly lady, dressed in black, possibly wearing a white blouse, with a large cameo brooch worn at her throat.'

Mrs Hardstone, anxious to know more about this haunting, contacted the last four tenants of the King's Head and all confirmed the presence of a ghost, though none knew of its origin. Comments Mrs Hardstone: 'I did not believe in anything like this when we came here but after the things that happened in the first three months, there is no doubt about its being haunted. There is no other explanation.'

The Headless Coachman

66 KING'S HEAD, Grafty Green, near Maidstone.
A Fremlin-Whitbread house on the road from Headcorn to Lenham. Open: 10 to 2.30 & 6 to 10.30. Friday and Saturday to 11. Sunday: 12 to 2 & 7 to 10.30. Snacks or Ceylon Curry only. Parking. Nearest station: Headcorn. Telephone: Ulcombe 259.

STAND FOR LONG enough at the door of this pub and you may see a phantom coach and pair driven by a headless coachman go hurtling towards Boughton Malherbe Church.

If you get tired of waiting go inside, order yourself a Ceylon Curry—they specialise in it here—and ask the landlord to introduce you to one man who can vouch for the ghost—a war-time Home Guard who heard it while returning from an evening on duty.

What he heard—the sound of bolting horses and the screams of terrified passengers—was a ghostly playback of what happened the day the four horses pulling the Lenham-bound coach took fright a few yards from the King's Head.

Out of control when it reached the church, the coach swung left off the road and into the drive of the Old Rectory, smashing into a giant chestnut tree. None of the passengers survived the impact. The coachman was catapulted from his box through the lower branches of the tree and decapitated.

None will dispute that the most colourful figure ever to drink at this picturesque pub is Dover Bill, a smuggler who called regularly with his gang. He left behind him, not a ghost but a feeling of hatred from 'shopping' his friends to the Revenue men, to save his own skin. He saw his gang hanged on Penenden Heath, outside Maidstone, after which he was ostracised by friends and neighbours and died at Grafty Green almost penniless.

The Discarded Boot

67 RINGLESTONE TAVERN, Harrietsham.
A free house on A20, the Maidstone to Ashford road. Open: 11.30 to 2.30 & 6 to 10.30. Sunday: 12 to 2 & 7 to 10.30. Lunches and dinner. No accommodation. Ample parking. Nearest station: Harrietsham. Telephone: Harrietsham 207.

THE INTERIOR of the 16th-century Ringlestone has not been changed since 1732. Its walls are still of the original natural brick which glows warmly when lit by candles and oil-lamps—as all the bars are. In winter blazing logs crackle and splutter in the great ingles, the reflected firelight dancing on the mirror-like surfaces of carved settles and varnished beams. Winter and summer the ghost walks, stomping up the cellar steps by night, halting at the top and removing one boot, which is thrown to the floor, but never taking off the other. Whoever he was--an intruder bent on robbery, a lover approaching a waiting mistress, or maybe the suspecting husband about to surprise the lovers—he was evidently stopped dead in his tracks.

The Burnt Woman

68 THE FOX AND HOUNDS, Canterbury Road, Herne Common.
A Shepherd Neame house on A291 about 2 miles south of Herne Bay. Open: 10 to 2.30 & 6 to 10.30. (Friday and Saturday to 11.) Sunday: 12 to 2 & 7 to 10.30. Parking. Nearest station: Herne Bay. Telephone: Herne Bay 4849.

PHIL BENNETT was a lad of 12 when he had his first encounter with the ghost of The Fox and Hounds.

His father was then the landlord of this pub, which in those pre-war days was semi-isolated on the road midway between Herne Bay and Canterbury.

Phil was a boarder at a not too distant Kent boarding school and went home at weekends 'to explore'—exploration which became more alarming than exciting.

In a tape recorded interview with Alan Reeve-Jones* he recalls his very first night at The Fox and Hounds:

'I went to bed and I was awakened in a manner that seemed to me to be unusual. I thought: now, something has woken me up.

---

* Alan Reeve-Jones is a Welshman with a tremendous sense of humour. It was he who wrote the Batsford guide *London Pubs* which is one of the most hilarious books I have read since *Three Men in a Boat*. He tape recorded Philip Bennett's experience in the late spring of 1970, shortly before Mr Bennett went to Australia.

'There, standing at the foot of the bed, an old-fashioned brass bedstead, was the extremely grotesque looking figure of a woman. I say grotesque because it was. The hands—I could see her hands very clearly—appeared as if they had all the flesh burnt off and the face was the same. She looked as though she'd been in a very severe fire.

'Now I didn't know this, until during the war, when we used to see pilots who'd suffered from fire in the cockpit. They looked like that. I suddenly remembered saying: "Ah, now I know, this is quite conclusive; she'd been very badly burned."

'On this first occasion I think my brother came in. He heard me calling for my mother but my parents used to sleep very solidly.'

Phil Bennett avoided sleeping at the pub after that. At weekends he stayed with friends whenever he could, though that was not always possible and during the time his father had The Fox and Hounds— about $2\frac{1}{2}$ years—he saw the ghost five times.

He recollects that his parents were not at all sympathetic about his experiences. He told Alan Reeve-Jones: 'I heard my mother talking to my father one day about me and about the fact that she had seen this thing. My father also said he had seen it, but it was nothing to worry about he said. It didn't do any harm and he dismissed it, like that, as irresponsible. But to me it was very, very real.'

Describing his experience in more detail he said: 'There were lots of trappings that went with this; quite the whole business. If you went upstairs you walked through a wall of cold. This was an area, very sharply defined, about three feet thick on the top landing. It wasn't a draught. Just an area of extreme drop in temperature. You could actually back into it and step into it. It was rather like going through swing doors. If that was on, then there would be the smell of burnt flowers, the sort of smell you get from flowers which have died and you are burning in the grate or something to get rid of them and they make an unpleasant smell. And sure enough, that night, you would have an experience.'

A Shotgun On The Bed

There was one afternoon when Phil met the ghost downstairs in the kitchen, when he was preparing tea at about 4.30. But the occasion which stands out in his memory is what he terms 'the final pay-off' when his father was about to give up The Fox and Hounds and he, having finished school, was faced with no alternative but to live at the pub for an entire fortnight.

'I had just had my 15th birthday,' recalls Mr Bennett. 'It was summer. I am a July man you see and, well, by this time I was in a bad state. I had a loaded shotgun on the bed—a .410—under the eiderdown. We had the full business of the smelling flowers and the cold wall and the thing I didn't like to mention is that this woman shook the bed. She shook it so severely that it made a terrible noise, and I used to think, surely somebody would hear this and come in.

'And I remember, during this, looking away at the floor and making a mental note of how much the bed moved during the shaking, marking the edge of the knobs against the window. Suddenly, I let fly with the shotgun. All the bullets went into the white wardrobe at the back, well at the head of the bed. Then my father came in, took the gun away from me. He was very sympathetic and very concerned. So was my mother.

'The ghost had disappeared but the smell hadn't. I can remember the smell even being outside the building. When I went and sat in the car I can remember remarking on it. I attached a lot of importance to this smell and I remember my mother saying "Yes, I can smell it as well." I said, "Well, mother, that's it" and she said, "I often smelled that."

'I sat in the car. It was half past three in the morning and my father made tea and pleaded with me to come back and go to bed but I didn't. I had to stay somewhere for the fortnight. He took me back to school. I thought I'd get told off by the brothers—very strict Catholics—but they never said a word and we left the place. That was in 1937.'

Not until 1964 did Mr Bennett go back to The Fox and Hounds. By then he was a veteran of World War II and skilled in the space-age science of electronics. His ghostly encounters were a thing of history.

The return visit is vivid in his memory. He remembers introducing himself to the landlady and coming straight to the point as she poured a glass of light ale:

'I said, "What about the ghost upstairs?" She put the glass down on the counter with quite a bang from the half poured bottle and said to her husband: "You come and hear what this customer has to say and now you tell me if you think our son is imagining things."

The Nun Upstairs

'The woman told me that the little boy was only nine or ten. She said the first time was when they'd only been there a short while and he came down to the bar and said "Oh mum, there's a nun upstairs, I think she wants to see you." The woman was most indignant about even a nun or a priest breaking into the house and going upstairs. This is unusual even for somebody of the cloth. Of course she went up there—and no nun. Now this child had a number of experiences. He reported this nun all over the place; outside the building, in the kitchen, upstairs in his room, generally all over.

'The daughter, aged 19, had never seen this ghost but had experienced the cold block and the smell of the burnt flowers.

'I came back again in 1967 and very bold, I thought, let's go in and see again. The woman said: "Oh please don't think I'm rude, but last time you were here all hell was let loose three hours afterwards. All the clothes were ripped off my husband's bed and we heard the most terrible noise from upstairs as though there were a couple of heavy-weight wrestlers fighting up there." And she said: "When we went up, all the drawers in the desk were pulled out and the papers strewn over the floor, and the bed was all unmade and swung around and everything was in a general mess.

"And there was this crate of bottles, or crates about 6 ft high which had been pulled over, breaking lots of the bottles and causing a lot of noise and general disturbance." She said, "Obviously somebody didn't like you here so please go away." Which I did. I left. Actually that quite alarmed me. I should have mentioned that in 1964 they invited me to go upstairs if I liked to and take a photograph, which I did. You know it was quite eerie going up there again, up to that bedroom.'

The Wall of Death

69 THE COOPER'S ARMS, Rochester.
A Courage house in St Margaret's Street. Open : 10 to 2.30 & 6 to 11.
Sunday : 12 to 2 & 7 to 10. Snacks and grills. No accommodation.
Parking. Nearest station : Rochester. Telephone : Medway 41052.

THIS PUB has a pedigree to be envied. It is thought to be the oldest in Kent—so old as to be listed in the Domesday Book—and has its own coat of arms. In the 11th century it was part of the priory—the brewery part. Cooper's tools used by the brothers for the making of their barrels can still be seen there . . . So can the ghost of one of the brethren who was walled up and left to die for committing some unforgivable sin. It is a shrouded, misty, grey figure which emerges from the wall of the bar and then disappears, leaving behind an intensely cold atmosphere. It manifests itself only once a year—usually in November and late at night.

The Restraining Influence

70 THE GEORGE, Rochester.
A Courage house in the High Street. Open : 10 to 2.30 & 6 to 11.
Sunday : 12 to 2 & 7 to 10. Snacks. Accommodation. Parking.
Nearest station : Rochester. Telephone : Medway 47697.

LIKE ITS NEAR neighbour in St Margaret Street, this pub is haunted by a monk, said by Mr Clyde Weldon, the landlord, to be 'a very old man, on the small side, but smiling.' Unlike the misty grey figure of the near-by Cooper's Arms, this ghost is described as 'solid.' He too haunts in the pub cellar which, in fact, is the crypt of what remains of a 14th-century church. From here there was once a tunnel giving access to Rochester Castle and the cathedral, though both passages have long been blocked and sealed off. It was not until repair work to the castle was being carried out recently that the ghost was first seen in the cellar of The George. One man who has not seen the ghost but felt it is a barman at the pub. When he was about to leave the cellar after changing over the barrels in use, he felt as if something or somebody was holding him back, making movement of his legs and arms almost impossible. For some minutes he was powerless to climb back up the cellar steps.

The Murdered Soldier

71 THE CHEQUERS, Smarden, near Ashford.
A Courage house in the village centre on B2077, Charing to Biddenden road. Open: 10 to 2.30 & 6 to 10.30. Sunday: 12 to 2 & 7 to 10.30. Lunches and dinner. Accommodation. Parking. Nearest station: Pluckley. Telephone: Smarden 217.

THE CHEQUERS is a 14th-century pub with a 19th-century ghost— that of a soldier home from the wars in Napoleon's France who was murdered for the fat purse he carried.

That is one story. But I have heard the soldier referred to as a French prisoner-of-war who was caught and killed while on the run from Sissinghurst Castle. Perhaps his habit of pacing impatiently backwards

Inn sign, Cardinal's Error, Tonbridge (No. 72)

and forwards between the two oldest bedrooms in the pub, is more the action of a hounded escapee. Either way, its presence starts the dogs howling. One dog, an Afghan hound, was so disturbed by the haunting that it had to have tranquillisers to calm its nerves.

The old part of the pub certainly has a strange atmosphere, say the regulars. It has a shady past too. A gang of sheep smugglers used it as their headquarters, gaining access by a tunnel from the village church and assuring themselves of a quick get-away with their woolly contraband through another tunnel which led from the inn to Ronden Castle, about a mile away.

Smarden, like its near neighbour, Pluckley, is one of Kent's much haunted villages. It can boast also of a wealth of half-timbered houses, mostly built by the Flemish weavers who settled and prospered in this delightful countryside of apple orchards and hopfields, which stretch out between the North and South Downs like a vast patchwork quilt.

Bed Sitter

72 CARDINAL'S ERROR, Tonbridge.
A Whitbread house in Lodge Oak Lane on the outskirts of the town. Open : 10.30 to 2.30 & 6 to 10.30. (Friday and Saturday to 11.) Sunday : 12 to 2 & 7 to 10.30. Ample parking. Snacks. Nearest station : Tonbridge. Telephone : Tonbridge 2032.

THE CARDINAL'S ERROR* has been a pub since 1946, but the building, with its low-beamed ceiling and mellowed tiles, is about 500 years old. It gets its name from Cardinal Wolsey's mistaken faith in Henry VIII. Wolsey suppressed Tonbridge Priory and promised a 'great grammar school' in its place. But before he could keep his promise to the people of Tonbridge the Cardinal had lost the king's favour. It is not Wolsey's ghost that haunts this pub but that of an unknown woman. The eldest daughter of the licensee complained one night of a lady in a large hat sitting at the bottom of her bed. A visitor to the inn had a similar experience.

According to one spiritualist who visited the house, the ghost that has from time to time caused noises in the night, or moved things around, 'is a friendly spirit.'

* Reprinted from *The Ghost Tour* published by Wolfe Publishing.

King's Head, Grafty Green (No. 66)

Lancashire

The Skull of the Roundhead

73 PACK HORSE INN, Affetside, near Bury.
A Hydes' Anvil house just off the Bolton to Ramsbottom road (A676).
Open : 11.30 to 3 & 5.30 to 10.30. Friday and Saturday to 11. Sunday :
12 to 2 & 7 to 10.30. Ample parking. No accommodation. Hot and
cold snacks. Nearest station : Bury. Telephone : Tottington 3802.

SKULLS, grinning and grisly, such as the one that looks down on you
as you sup your ale at the bar of the Pack Horse, are common enough
ornaments in some English houses. There is one not so very far away
at Wardley Hall and another at Burton Agnes near Bridlington. Bettis-
combe Manor in Dorset had a reputation as the house of the Screaming
Skull, while Warbleton Priory Farm tucked away in deepest Sussex had,
not one, but two skulls—those of a former owner of the house and
the man who murdered him.

Nearly all these skulls, including the one at the Pack Horse, have one
thing in common; their original owners left behind them a death-bed
threat that their skull be preserved and never removed from its leering
place of horror—or else.

Or else what? Well, in the case of Wardley Hall, when the gruesome
relic was once given a proper Christian burial 'a terrible tempest shook
the house until it seemed about to fall and all the barns and outhouses
were unroofed.' On another occasion when the old place was down
on its luck and let out as tenements, an attempt was made to get rid
of the skull, 'but there was no peace in the house until it was restored.'

Similar stories are told about Burton Agnes Hall and, say the legend
lovers, if you move the skull from this Affetside pub there will be
hell to pay. So there it stays, the skull of George Whewell, a man from
Affetside who, during the Civil War, beheaded James, the seventh Earl
of Derby and who was in turn executed by the Royalists.

Skull or no skull, this 15th-century inn is worth a visit for the view
alone. Pollution permitting, you can see for miles since this is the
highest point of old Watling Street, the military highway engineered
by the Romans in A.D. 79 to connect Manchester with Ribchester.

Step across the road to where the cross stands by the wayside and
you will be at the halfway point between London and Edinburgh.

The Dunkley Boggart

74   DUNKENHALGH HOTEL, Clayton-le-Moors, near Accrington.
An 'Old English' hotel standing in its own grounds. Open : 10.30 to 3 & 5.30 to 11. Sunday : 11.30 to 2 & 7 to 10.30. Accommodation : 29 bedrooms. Lunch and dinner. Parking. Nearest station : Accrington (5 mls.). Telephone : Accrington 34333.

THE PETRE children adored Lucette. She was not just another governess. She was French and she was young and laughed a lot; what is more, she would listen to all their childish problems as though they really did matter. She was so different from other governesses they'd had. They were not alone in thinking that; most of the Petre household thought so too.

The Petre family had married into Dunkenhalgh Park when Robert Petre made 16-year-old Catherine Walmesley his wife, at the beginning of the 18th century. She had inherited the estate on which Judge Walmesley, old Sir Thomas, her great-grandfather, had spent a fortune, building and enlarging a century earlier.

The grounds of the big house in those days stretched for miles. There were 600 acres of deer park where Lucette took the children walking and where she gave them their lessons under the great oaks and beeches. A favourite place was the yew walk or down by the old stone bridge under which the River Hyndburn flows—the place where Lucette's ghost haunts today.

Older folk in Clayton-le-Moors still refer to the old 'Boggart Bridge' and, from somewhere deep in their memories recall snatches of the story they were told as children about Lucette's love affair with a young Redcoat officer back from the wars in Europe. He was one of the family at Dunkenhalgh, home for Christmas, a gay devil-may-care fellow who overwhelmed Lucette with flattery and charm. She found him irresistible. When the feasting was over, he rode away to rejoin King George's army, leaving her with the promise of marriage when he returned in the spring.

Tormented Lucette

By high summer she was obviously pregnant and in despair. Although the Petre family were understanding, Lucette found the backstairs whispering and the gossip hard to bear. She would walk in the park under the trees and beside the river, hoping not to meet the children, hiding if she saw them coming. Life at Dunkenhalgh was becoming impossible, yet she dared not go home to France. It was a dilemma that drove her to distraction. In a demented moment at the height of a summer storm, she ran to the river and threw herself into the swollen waters. The next morning her body was taken from among the reeds downstream, wrapped in a shroud and carried back to the big house.

Had she been able to live with her tormented self a few weeks more she would have been able to marry her soldier lover. He came back, unaware of what had happened and faced Lucette's brother in a duel. He died, an officer and almost a gentleman, at the end of a savage rapier thrust.

There was a time when the grandfathers of quite a few of those now living at Clayton-le-Moors would talk of the 'Dunkley Boggart,' as they called it, with hushed voices. There were folk who wouldn't pass the big house after dark without a shudder, and certainly not at Christmas. For then it is that Lucette's ghost is seen, dressed in a shroud, drifting silently among the trees, walking by the river and disappearing as she crosses the old stone bridge.

The Cross on the Ceiling

75 NEW INN, Foulridge, near Colne.
A Thwaites house two miles north of Colne on the A56 road to Skipton. Open : 11 to 3 & 5.30 to 10.30. No accommodation. Serves snacks. Parking. Nearest station : Colne. Telephone : Colne 895.

THE DAY CROMWELL halted his army on the moor above Colne he looked out over the rain-swept Craven Valley towards Pendle Hill and made a snap decision. 'This is a foul ridge to fight on; we'll do battle down there,' he told his men. Which not only won him the day but gave the village its name.

That was 322 years ago, when this pub, a square built place of stone and slate on an island of cobbles, actually was 'The New Inn.'

Years later when the Quakers were strong in these parts a Friends Meeting House went up on an adjoining site and they buried their dead in a graveyard which is now a garden on the west side of the inn. Headstones from the overgrown graves were used to build the surrounding wall and though it was suggested at the time that the bones be re-interred, it was never done.

When in the mid-1960's the New Inn was given a face lift, the landlord and his wife moved into a small back bedroom while the work went on.

'We just had to leave it in the end,' comments the landlord. 'Something or someone used to come knocking at the bedroom door, usually around one in the morning. The police could find no evidence of a break-in. Anyway, at that time the front door was nailed up with six-inch nails and the back door was bolted. Strangely enough, the dog, which slept at my feet, never seemed to be disturbed.'

But the family who lived at the New Inn at the turn of the century was disturbed not only by the knocking but also by a luminous cross which appeared at night on the ceiling of the same small back room, occupied then by two young brothers.

The Lass of Bridge House

76   THE BRIDGE HOUSE, Hapton.
A Thwaites house in the village of Hapton, 2½ miles from Accrington. Open: 10.30 to 3 & 6 to 10.30. Friday & Saturday 11. Sunday: 12 to 2 & 7 to 10.30. Snacks. Limited parking. Nearest station: Hapton. Telephone: Burnley 72473.

THE LEEDS and Liverpool Canal slices through the heart of Hapton like the tarnished blade of a giant knife. This grey, still waterway was once busy with barges, its banks ringing to the clip-clopping of horses straining at the end of towropes.

Behind The Bridge House the bargees had their stable and a yard from which wooden steps led up to the pub's back door, convenient for a quick pint when the going had been hard. There were times when the stables were used for a more macabre purpose, as a mortuary for those who chose the canal as a way out of their troubles. Some of the older customers at the Bridge House can recall the details of a local lass who flung herself from the canal bridge and whose ghost has since returned to haunt the pub.

One winter night in 1954, Mr J P Donohue, the then licensee of The Bridge House, encountered this ghost. It was ten minutes past closing time and snowing hard outside. Mr Donohue had cleared up in the bar and gone into his living room to give his dog some food. To do this he had to pass the open door of the pantry and as he went by he noticed a woman going up the steps at the far end. He knew the steps led to nowhere else except the pantry so assumed it was his wife getting the supper. Having attended to the dog he called to his wife, thinking she was still in the pantry but was surprised to find that she was not there and had not been near the pantry all the evening.

In the bar next day, still puzzled by his experience, he talked to the builders who at that time were converting the old stables into toilets. He questioned his customers, especially the older ones among the regulars. They told him stories their fathers and grandfathers had often recounted of the thriving days of the Leeds and Liverpool Canal. It was then that he heard for the first time of previous tenant's who'd met the ghost of the Lass of Bridge House in similar circumstances.

A Presence on the Stairway?

77   BLACK BULL, Huncoat.
A Thwaites house on the Burnley to Accrington road (A679). Open: 11.30 to 3 & 5 to 10.30. Sunday: 12 to 2 & 7 to 10.30. Snacks at bar. Parking. Nearest station: Huncoat. Telephone: Accrington 36428.

A 16TH-CENTURY INN on the Burnley road where the Cromwellian army is said to have halted for refreshment. Haunted by the inexplicable ringing of the bar service bells in the night.

'We had the wiring checked after the first disturbance but found no fault' say the brewers.

The landlady has the feeling that someone or something haunts the stairs and when she goes up them she finds it impossible to look round to see who is behind her—though not through fear. Her dogs are reluctant to go downstairs alone or at times even if accompanied by their owner.

Highwayman's Haunt

78 PUNCH BOWL, Hurst Green, near Blackburn.
A Dutton's house, 6 miles from Clitheroe on the B6243 road to Longridge. Open: 11 to 3 & 5.30 to 11, with an hour's supper extension. No accommodation. Nearest station: Blackburn (10 mls.). Telephone: Stonyhurst 209.

NED KING was a highwayman when the 18th century was in its teens. He was not as well up in the highwaymen's league as Dick Turpin, simply because he did not roam so far afield. He confined his talents as a gentleman of the road to the ten miles of wild Lancashire countryside between Longridge and Clitheroe.

When King was a lad the Punch Bowl at Hurst Green was a farmhouse and a cluster of cottages. It became an inn in 1793. A few years later King, a rugged, good-looking man in his twenties, was making the Punch Bowl his headquarters, watching potential victims from the safety of the hayloft above the barn, sizing up the moneyed gentry and their perfumed ladies when they came in on the coach.

When they went on their way replete and heady with wine, King— a dashing figure in white ruffled shirt and gold-trimmed scarlet coat, white riding breeches and knee-high black boots—was waiting for them with pistols cocked, a mile or so along at the bend in the road.

His escape route across the fields back to the Punch Bowl is today a pleasant Sunday afternoon walk for the boys of Stonyhurst College. In fact, generations of Stonyhurst pupils have had their farewell 'dos' at the Punch Bowl.

Ned King's farewell 'do' was as packed with drama as the rest of his short life. He was finally run to earth in his favourite hide-out—the loft above the barn, now the inn's dining-room. He shot it out with the troopers who had him cornered at a spot which is roughly the right-hand corner of the restored Minstrels' Gallery. King was overpowered and put in chains.

There is no record of a trial at either Blackburn or Preston, but local historians say he was subsequently hanged from the gibbet at the edge of Gallows Lane, no more than an all-out gallop from the old inn's front door.

Many times must King have galloped past that grim spot en route to another holdup and many times since his ghost has probably passed that way returning to the Punch Bowl.

The inn suffered much inconvenience from King's ghost for a hundred years or more after he was hanged. In 1942 a priest from Stonyhurst College performed an exorcism. Since when the hauntings have become less frequent although there have been instances of bottles unaccountably falling off shelves, unexplained noises along the corridors and a moaning among the rafters which is not caused by the wind blowing off Longridge Fell.

The receptionist at Hurst Green's Punch Bowl says: 'I wouldn't stay the night alone in this place for anything. I can't explain what it is. It's something to do with the atmosphere in the place. It changes at night and you feel as though there's someone—something—here that you can't put your finger on. It's eerie.'

The resident manager, an ex-Merchant Navy man, says: 'I am a pretty hard-boiled character. It wouldn't bother me if I had to sleep here on my own for a month. I'll take my chances with any ghostly highwayman who might be knocking around. History says he was rather a bad-tempered sort of ghost making a lot of noise when things didn't go his way. That's why he was exorcised.'

The Rocking Chair

79 SHAKESPEARE HOTEL, Fountain Street, Manchester, 2.
A Watney house in the city centre. Open: 11 to 3 & 5.30 to 10.30. Sunday: 12 to 2 & 7 to 10.30. Lunches. No parking. Station: Manchester (Piccadilly). Telephone: 061/832/4844 or 4043.

EVERY CITY has its show biz pub, a home from home, for the acting profession. In Manchester, appropriately enough, it is the Shakespeare, which is a centuries-old inn surrounded by a forest of concrete and glass in the new city centre.

Mr Martyn Das, who has now given up dancing his way round the world after a lifetime of cabaret and exhibition performances, stayed often at the Shakespeare. To him the resident ghost is virtually as much an old acquaintance as Frank Cork and his wife, who first introduced him to the haunting when they were running the place in the years after World War II. Mr Das never tires of talking about this ghost because, he says, 'before encountering it I did not believe in such happenings at all, but having seen all the circumstances surrounding the story I can and do believe it.

'The inn has a very large kitchen, as would be necessary to feed some 10 to 15 guests, plus lunches served in the pub itself,' says Mr Das. 'There are several large electric stoves and several large fridges, and in one corner an outsize rocking chair, which is a strange thing to find in a hotel kitchen. A flight of about ten wooden stairs lead up to a small room, used for storing food, eggs and such like.'

There was a time when this small room was used by the hotel kitchen maid of a hundred years ago. She slept there in order to be up in the very early hours to see to the fires under the cooking ranges. She undressed and went to bed by candle light and on one occasion, too exhausted to know what she was doing, caught her clothes alight. In a panic she rushed to the top of the stairs and fell headlong to her death. It is thought to be her ghost that has been seen by both staff and guests.

'I remember one night when the drummer at the Cabaret Club saw this girl standing at the top of the stairs,' recalls Mr Das. 'Some have seen the rocking chair start to rock although nobody was sitting in it at the time. Several of the staff claimed to have seen it moving back and forth of its own accord. Years previously there were gas stoves in the kitchen and on a number of occasions these were found turned on although it was in the middle of the night and nobody had been in the kitchen since supper. That's the reason the electric stoves were installed.'

The Sad Cavalier

80 THE RING O' BELLS, Middleton, near Manchester.
A John W. Lee's house in the town centre. Open: 11 to 3 & 5.30 to 10.30 (Friday & Saturday 11). Sunday: 12 to 2 & 7 to 10.30. Snacks at bar. Parking (in Church Square). Nearest station: Manchester (6 mls.). Telephone: 061/643/3041.

THIS IS ONE of those pubs whose fame as a haunted inn has spread to America. In fact I first heard about it from folk in Seattle, who, before visiting Britain, wrote asking if the ghost of the Sad Cavalier was still haunting The Ring o' Bells. It is. Over the years the Cavalier has been seen dressed in plumed hat, lace collar and cloak and carrying a sword. It is described by the landlady as 'a friendly ghost, but sad looking.' Many times unexplained footsteps have been heard in the cellar . . . Excavations in the cellar and the tunnels leading from it have uncovered helmets and a variety of 17th-century weapons.

The cellars date back to the Normans, but bones found under the flagstones are thought to be those of the Cavalier who was killed by Roundheads in the parish church across the road. It is the ghost of that murdered Royalist who is said to haunt the pub, which is Middleton's oldest building. Like the parish church, The Ring o' Bells had its beginning in Saxon times. In all probability the chaps who built the original church also built the original Ring o' Bells, though it is hard to say which came first; the pub most likely, since building can be thirsty work.

Leicestershire

Five-to-Four Fred

81 THE BELPER ARMS, Newton Burgoland.
A Watney house, 3 miles west of Ibstock (A447). Open : 10.30 to 2.30 & 6 to 10.30 (Saturday 11). Sunday : 12 to 2 & 7 to 10.30. Snacks, lunches and dinner. Bed and breakfast. Street parking. Nearest station : Atherstone, Warks. (12 mls.). Telephone : Measham 05307/70530.

NO ONE has ever actually seen the ghost of The Belper Arms, but many have felt it.

It has a liking for women, caressing their faces with a soft, affectionate touch, or, more saucily, slapping their bottoms.

So it must surely be the ghost of a man, a devil-may-care fellow with an eye for the girls and a particularly aggressive trait towards men. They get very different treatment—a cold pair of hands clasped across the nose and mouth as if to suffocate them.

Because this ghost usually makes its presence felt at about five to four in the morning or afternoon, it has become known at The Belper as 'Five-to-Four-Fred.' His presence is made apparent by a drop in temperature; though there may be a big fire blazing in the open hearth, the room becomes intensely cold.

A friend of the landlord's daughter, sleeping one night in the bar, was woken by this feeling of cold. This, and the feeling of being suffocated, resulted in his moving out to spend the remainder of the night in his car.

The ghost seems to dislike change and becomes particularly active whenever the pub is altered in any way. Its first manifestation was when an old wooden spiral staircase was removed from the 12th-century pub in 1962. Many times since, one regular in particular, sitting on a settle near to where the staircase was sited, has encountered 'Five-to-Four-Fred,' feeling the clasping hands across his face and only able to breathe after going outside.

The landlord and his wife and daughter have all felt the ghost's presence. They have encountered it during the night 'as though a cat is walking over the bed' said the landlord's wife, 'even though one cannot see anything there.'

A cleaner they employed felt it more forcibly than most with a slap on the bottom. Since she left more indignant than frightened, other cleaners have experienced the same thing.

Parts of this pub are more than 700 years old, more ancient than the church, in the tiny village, which is no more than an arrow's flight from Bosworth Field, where King Richard III did battle for the last time in 1485.

Originally the house was used by the masons who built the church. It is the first item noted in the village records. Curiously, the newer part of the pub, which is only 250 years old, is not haunted, which suggests that this ghost had its origin before 1700, in the days when the original pub was a small isolated cottage inn known as The Shepherd and Shepherdess.

For years it was known to the locals and travellers as The Halfway House, a name it earned by being on one of the main coaching roads out of Leicester, a notorious road for highwaymen, from Turpin down.

Lincolnshire

Henry Keeps on Walking

32 ABBEY HOSTEL HOTEL, Crowland.
*An Allied Breweries house on East Street. Open : 10.30 to 2.30 & 6 to
10.30. Friday and Saturday : 6 to 11. Sunday : 12 to 2 & 7 to 11.
Accommodation. Snacks at bar. Lunch and dinner. Parking.
Nearest station : Peterborough. Telephone : Crowland 200.*

ON THE MORNING of February 1, 1844, Henry Girdlestone started
walking. Being a farmer he was dressed in farmer's clothes and carried
a heavy walking stick. On his feet was a pair of stout-soled boots and
at his side trotted a small terrier dog.

Henry was well known in the Fens for his toughness and his readiness
to accept a challenge, especially if it was coupled with a worthwhile
wager. That's how he came to be starting out on this long walk, one of
the most astonishing feats of physical endurance ever performed by
an individual.

Even beside today's remarkable accomplishments—sailing round the
world single-handed, rowing the Atlantic, trekking across the North
Pole—the thought of Henry Girdlestone's marathon leaves one gasping.

It left a good number of people gasping that night in the Abbey
Hostel Hotel at Crowland when he boasted that if the occasion should
arise he could and would walk a thousand miles.

The friends with whom he was drinking urged him not to be so foolish,
but Henry persisted. Not only would he walk a thousand miles on his
own two legs if challenged to do so, but he'd walk the distance in a
given time, say a thousand consecutive hours.

Practically everybody in the Abbey Hostel on that memorable evening
challenged him. Several books were started and betting was fast and
furious. When the last few pence had been staked it was agreed that
Henry should begin his walk the following week.

At first the young farmer strode along the flat Lincolnshire countryside fairly casually. Sometimes he walked only a mile an hour, taking a
rest whenever he was ahead of his timetable. Slowly the stumpy spire
of Crowland Abbey disappeared from view and he walked on and on.

After he'd covered about 200 miles his terrier began to limp, but not
Henry. He strode on, often accompanied by a cluster of people from

villages on his route. They gave him food and water, stayed with him for a few miles and then with a word of encouragement left him to plod on. And it was becoming a plod. After about twenty days he seemed to be walking in a trance. After thirty days his condition was causing some concern and those who had challenged him offered to withdraw their bets and call the whole thing off.

Henry Girdlestone was made of sterner stuff than they had bargained for and refused to give up. Though he sometimes walked with his eyes closed as if asleep on his feet, he seldom faltered. He never left the road or missed his way and 49 days after he set out he stumbled up to the door of the Abbey Hostel, and sank to the ground exhausted. He had walked 1,025 miles 173 yards to win a sizeable fortune as well as the congratulations of friends and villagers for miles around.

As news of his achievement spread farm hands stopped work in the fields and hurried to the inn to toast Henry's success. Henry had a hot bath, a good meal, a gallon of ale and was finally carried to bed to sleep like a log for three whole days.

But since his death—some long time after his marathon—Henry Girdlestone has gone on walking at the Abbey Hostel Hotel. He sometimes walks all night along the corridors of the attic. At times the footsteps falter as though the walker was very weary.

Nobody claims to have seen the ghost but it is generally agreed that, judging by the sound, Henry is still wearing the thick-soled boots he had on that day in 1844.

London

Charlie Takes the Blame

**83 THE ANCHOR TAP, Horselydown Lane,
Bermondsey, S.E.1.**
*A Courage house on the south side of Tower Bridge. Open: 11 to 3
& 5.30 to 11. Sunday: 12 to 2 & 7 to 10.30. Lunches Monday to
Friday. Snacks at weekend. Nearest station: London Bridge or
Tower Hill (underground). London Transport buses Nos. 42 and 78
pass the door. Telephone: 407/2280.*

'SOME VERY funny things go on in this pub—and there's no explanation to any of them,' says Mrs Phyllis Chandler, the wife of the
licensee of The Anchor Tap. Things disappear and turn up in the
oddest of places—and 'Charlie' the ghost gets the blame. A short
while ago Mrs Chandler left a watch on her dressing-table when she
went to bed. In the morning she was unable to find it. 'Two months
later,' she says, 'I found that watch in the middle of some ironing in
the laundry cupboard. It was still ticking.'

The Lady and The Bull

84 THE BULL, Shooter's Hill, S.E.18.
*A Courage house on A207 half a mile east of Eltham Common.
Open: 11 to 3 & 5.30 to 11. Sundays: 12 to 2 & 7 to 10.30. Sandwiches
at bar. No accommodation. Parking. Nearest station: Welling (SR).
Telephone: 854/0582.*

FOR YEARS it was thought that there was some connection between
the White Lady of Shooter's Hill and The Bull. It was a story started
in 1881 when the last vestige of the Old Bull Hotel, which had stood on
the opposite side of the road since 1749 was demolished. A pistol,
elaborately chased, was found hidden in a sealed off part of the cellar.
Local residents allied this find with the discovery years before of the
skeleton of a woman found by a labourer digging near the top of
Shooter's Hill. The skull had been fractured by a blunt weapon and the
hair, still painstakingly braided, had adhered to the skull at the place
of impact.

Doubtless, said the rumour-makers, the pistol butt had been used to kill the woman and then the weapon concealed in the cellar. Although the woman was never identified and there is not a shred of real evidence to link the two incidents, there were those who believed that the ghost of a woman in a white dress encountered on Shooter's Hill in the 1830's was that of the dead woman with the braided hair.

When the Woman in White was first reported the Old Bull had long been closed as a hotel. Its heyday as the place where the officers of the former Woolwich garrison held their never-to-be-forgotten military banquets and lavish balls, had passed. By 1820 the officers had their own mess in the town and the Old Bull had become a boarding school.

All the same the present Bull, which was built across the road, is haunted, though not by the White Lady. Judging by the noise this ghost makes as it moves across the room above the lounge bar and down the stairs, it is no lady. Heavy deliberate footsteps have been heard at various times by the customers and by the manager and his wife. Once at midday those drinking in the lounge put down their pints to listen to the ghost walking above their heads. On another occasion it was 2.30 in the morning when a friend waiting for the family to return from a night out, heard the ghostly steps coming down the stairs, stopping only when they reached the last tread.

Mrs Weedon, the wife of the manager (in 1970) well remembers the day she was serving her young daughter and a friend with a meal when she got a vivid impression of someone's face close to hers. But the impression was so fleeting that she was not able to describe the features.

A Ghost in Dockland

85 CONNAUGHT TAVERN, Connaught Road, E.16.
A Truman's house at the entrance to the Royal Albert Docks in London's East End. Open: 9.45 to 3 & 5.30 to 10.30 (Saturday 11). Sunday: 12 to 2 & 7 to 10.30. Snacks. Restricted parking. Nearest station: Plaistow (underground) then by 41 or 249 bus (London Transport). Telephone: 476/1886.

JACK DASH, the Dockers' leader, spoke outside this pub on many a damp, grey half-dawn and on many another occasion too. One of his performances resulted in the Connaught claiming the record for selling the most hogsheads of bitter in one lunchtime. That was in the mid-60's when Jack Dash held a meeting at the gates of the Royal Albert Dock and the parched throats of 7,000 supporters needed lubrication.

Because the Connaught is hard by the dock gates, the customers are men off the ships as well as those who work at unloading them, though the notice outside the pub says 'This house is open for the sale of intoxicants from six to eight of the clock in the morning to persons following the lawful trade of dockers.' That early morning licence

The Connaught Tavern, Connaught Road (No. 85)

127

granted to the pub when it was opened in 1884, ceased in 1971 when the Dockers' charter put an end to the use of casual labour—and put an end to the big takings. When young Mr Offord—Richard Offord, at 24 one of the youngest landlords in the trade—ran the Connaught a half a dozen years back he took anything up to £3,000 a week on beer alone.

But it was not always like that. On the customers' side of the bar there is at least one man who can vividly recall the desperate days that led up to the General Strike, when, to keep a fire burning in the pub grate, sleepers were ripped up from the railway track opposite.

That was only a few years before a young man of 22 by the name of Helms went to work at the Connaught. He worked as a barman and, with three other lads, lived in. It was part of his job to open the pub doors at 6 o'clock every morning in readiness for the breakfast trade.

Mr Helms, now retired and living in South East London, remembers:

'The ground floor was living quarters. The first floor was the boss's sitting room and bedroom and for the staff. The second floor had been the living quarters of the boss's old aunt and was never used. Nobody ever went up to that floor. Right opposite the stairs leading up to the second floor was a bedroom in which the boss's aunt went mad and committed suicide.

'Nobody would go near there, particularly at night, but I ventured in with two other lads, Tom and Charlie, to find the room in absolute chaos. The bed had never been made and the bed clothes were grey with dirt. I remember it all so plainly, even the pane of glass that was broken in the window.

'As we came out of the room, I was facing the stairs, and it was then that I saw the apparition of a woman, rather aged looking with a savage look about it. We were terrified and fled down the stairs. Call it imagination if you like but it was there all right, I can assure you. There were two Alsatian dogs, a mother and son, and they were as scared as we were of that room.'

Black Mother Marnes

86 YE OLDE GATEHOUSE, Highgate, N.6.
A Watney house at top of Highgate Hill. Open : 11 to 3 & 5.30 to 11. Sunday : 12 to 2 & 7 to 10.30. Snacks and lunches. Nearest station : Highgate underground. London Transport buses Nos. 210 and 271 pass the door. Telephone : 340/2154.

A PUB which dates back to 1310, when the then Bishop of London granted these premises their original licence, has almost a right to be haunted. This one, at the top of Highgate Hill, where there was a toll-gate until 1890, has a ghosted minstrels' gallery, once described by a visiting medium as 'a cold and evil place.'

The gallery, overlooking the modern ballroom, is the old part of the

ub, and here walks the ghost of Mother Marnes, a widow who, with
er cat, was murdered for her money. The ghost, a black, robed figure,
 said to appear only when there are no children or animals on the
remises. Which is probably why a previous landlord, Mr Robert
ilton, never saw it; his two children were forever going up to the
allery looking for shades of Mother Marnes. An earlier landlord who
id see the ghost had to have hospital treatment for shock, and later
ave up the tenancy on his doctor's advice.

Since then a stranger phenomenon has been reported by members
f the staff who, when looking in a particular mirror, do not see their
wn reflections but a blurred and cloudy image that is not recognisable.

AME NOTE: Toll gates did not come into general use until the passing
f the Turnpikes Act in 1663, but in 1364 Edward III authorised William
hillipe, a hermit, to set up a toll-bar on Highgate Hill. With the money
ollected from travellers, mostly drovers and graziers* on their way to
mithfield, he was ordered to keep the road in good repair.

he Menacing Grenadier

THE GRENADIER, Wilton Row, S.W.1.
*A Watney house. Open: 11 to 3 & 5.30 to 11. Sundays: 12 to 2 &
7 to 10.30. Open for lunch until 3 and for dinner until 11. Nearest
station: Hyde Park Corner (underground). Telephone: 235/3074
and 3400.*

UCKED AWAY behind St George's Hospital, barely out of earshot
f the endless snarl of traffic that swirls around Hyde Park Corner, is a
elightful survivor of the London of the early 1800's.

The worn stone steps which lead to the door of The Grenadier were
ounted by the elite young officers of the Duke of Wellington's
egiment, for in those tumultuous days this was their Mess. Most of the
uildings hereabouts had something to do with the army or the horses
at carried the army into battle.

There's an archway near-by that was part of the stables and a stone
hich was part of the Duke's mounting block. The alley which runs
eside the pub leading from Knightsbridge into Wilton Row is named
ld Barrack Yard: it was the yard in which Wellington's troops did their
quare-bashing. Here on a warm morning in June, 1815 they assembled
 all their polished splendour before leaving to fight at Waterloo.

In those days the pub was called The Guardsman. The public drank
elow stairs in what is now the cellar, while on the floor above them
e gentlemen of the regiment ate more than their fill, drank too much
nd gambled beyond their means. The gambling often led to cheating;
e cheating led to brawls and, in one of these, a young subaltern was
illed.

But there is a story that this grenadier was flogged to death after

See also *The Horns*, page 131.

The Grenadier, Wilton Row (No. 87)

130

being tried by a kangaroo court and 'sentenced' to be stripped and thrashed. Whichever way he died it was a violent end and presumably happened in September, since that is when his ghost walks.

Successive landlords of The Grenadier have reported unusual happenings. One said that the house had a peculiar, menacing atmosphere which built up through the year to reach its climax in September, and during that month he noticed that his dogs behaved strangely, showing signs of unrest; growling, snarling and sometimes scratching and digging in the cellar, which was probably the place where the body was concealed.

The same landlord's wife, changing in her bedroom, believing herself to be alone, left the door open and was annoyed when only half dressed, she saw the figure of a man coming up the stairs. But she was not able to recognise him and the figure vanished before it reached the top of the stairs.

Visitors drinking in the bar have seen the ghostly grenadier going upstairs, while one boyhood friend of the landlord who stayed the night at the pub said next morning that he was kept awake by the feeling that somebody was standing by the bed trying to touch him.

The landlord's son, lying in bed' with the door open, complained of the shadow of a person reflected on the bedroom wall from the landing —where a light had been left on—growing larger, then smaller, as if advancing and retreating, as if someone were pacing up and down outside in the corridor.

Ghost apart, this pub has received a great deal of attention since the days when George IV used it as his local and caused *The Times* to comment indignantly.

In more recent years it has been used for films, including *Around the World in Eighty Days*. It was the centre of a court case that resulted in the stopping of direct access of cars to the pub. The landlord, with a good eye for publicity introduced a rickshaw service.

One thing remains unaltered. In summer the long-established grapevine snaking out of the cobblestones still decorates The Grenadier's front door with a shady canopy of green.

The Screaming Child

48 THE HORNS, Crucifix Lane, S.E.1.
A Courage house, five minutes walk from Southwark Cathedral. Open 11 to 3 & 5.30 to 11. Snacks at the bar. No accommodation and no parking. Nearest station: London Bridge (underground), Northern Line, London Transport buses pass the door. Telephone: 407/2977.

CRUCIFIX LANE is no tourist Mecca, unless one has a fondness for soot-caked railway arches. It is a short, narrow street of dark factories on the one side, and on the other, built in to the arches, dismal warehouses, above which 500 trains a day clatter in and out of that draughty cavern called London Bridge station.

The commuter, riding cattle fashion in one of those rush hour trains, can look down in passing and see The Horns rubbing shoulders with Thompsons the box and paper bag makers. No doubt he will dismiss it as just another nondescript pub in that hotch-potch of bricks and mortar known as Bermondsey; but that would be because he would not know about the pub's resident ghost or how the noisy, fume-laden street that passes its door came to have such an incongruous name.

There was a time, 150 years back, when this part of Bermondsey had as its nearest neighbour Jacob's Island, a notorious place of open sewers and tidal ditches spanned by plank bridges. To the scum of London it was home, a rookery of slum dwellings perched on rotting platforms tottering above the black mud.

In the stinking water of the adjacent creek—ironically named St Saviours and today an area of deserted flour mills and tea warehouses awaiting the bulldozer—witches and whores were ducked to purge their souls.

The Holy Rood, from the old Bermondsey Abbey of St Saviours, set up at the junction of Bermondsey Street and Crucifix Lane, gave the lane its name. But nobody appears to know why The Horns was so-called, unless it was the favoured stop of the Kent drovers who around the 1820's were using Crucifix Lane as a short cut to the new bridge at Southwark, which lead directly to the markets of Eastcheap and Smithfield. This was the place they stopped for a last noggin on the way in and a real skinful on the way back.

The Horns was a common name for a pub frequented by drovers, graziers, shepherds and the like. Nearly every inn with this name used to keep a magnificent pair of horns, sometimes silver-tipped, for a curious custom of 'swearing on the horns,' a kind of initiation ceremony.

This originated as the swearing-in of drovers or graziers to their particular club at their favourite pub. They would kiss the horns of an ox or a ram that was brought to the door; by so doing they hoped to exclude strangers or undesirables who happened to have put up at the inn for the night.

That was how it all began—but it didn't stop there. Coach travellers seized on the ceremony as the in-thing to do. It became as popular with those abroad on the roads of Georgian England as crossing-the-line later became with globe-trotting Victorians.

The poet Byron took the oath of allegiance to The Horns at The Gatehouse,* Highgate, and summed up the ceremony in these lines:

> And many to the steep of Highgate hie,
> Ask ye, Bœotian shades! the reason why
> 'T's to the worship of the solemn horn,
> Grasp'd in the holy hand of mystery,
> In whose dread name both men and maids are sworn,
> And consecrate the oath with draught and dance till morn.

* See page 128.

While The Horns at Bermondsey cannot brag of a visit from the poet Byron, it can boast of a haunting almost as melodramatic as anything subsequently penned by the writers of Victorian parlour poetry.

The Wrights—Daphne Wright and her brother—were the tenants at The Horns when I first heard about the haunting.

'Our ghost does not appear,' said Miss Wright: 'It's a voice, the voice of a female child crying and calling for her mother. The age, we think, is about eight or ten. It was first heard about six years ago but was then thought to be a thing of the imagination. Since then the cries have become so frequent that five different people have heard them on separate occasions and two at one and the same time.'

Mrs Lauren Crutchley, of Bow, slept in the room 'in which I heard a young girl crying and sometimes screaming, not for her mother, but as if in fear of her mother. The voice was loud as if someone was shouting at me.'

Mrs Crutchley was in the public bar when next she heard the child crying. 'I asked those with me if they heard it too, and they said no, yet the voice was both distinctive and insistent, as though demanding help,' she said. 'I know I am not mistaken, I do believe I really heard it and not just imagined it.'

The Talking Ghost

In the summer of 1970 the Wrights gave up the tenancy of The Horns but before leaving Crucifix Lane Miss Wright wrote to me about the ghost of the crying child. This is what she wrote:

'Over the past few months the ghost we told you about has made her presence known more frequently, so much so that our cook was beginning to hear her. She would hear her talking on the stairs or calling her dog whereas previously we had been the only people to hear her. We decided then that as she seemed to be so desperately unhappy we would try to do something for her. So I wrote to the Bishop of Southwark who passed my letter on to Canon Pearce-Higgins* and that gentleman came down with a medium.

'We thought we had only the one ghost, but according to the medium we have two—the little girl and a very old lady. Apparently she is the one who is doing the banging and moving the furniture around and, just lately, sleeping in my brother's bed when he is not there.

'The Canon held Holy Communion, and then the medium went into a trance. He then led the little girl all the way down the stairs and out of the front door and assured us she would be all right. Apparently the child, whose name is thought to be Mary Isaac, once lived here. Her mother left her but came back for her when she was ill. She took her away but died soon after. The little girl died also but could not find her mother so she came back here in spirit form to look for her.

---

* Canon John Pearce-Higgins is internationally known for his work in freeing haunted houses of their ghosts. He is a Canon and Vice-Provost of Southwark Cathedral and Vice-Chairman of the Church's Fellowship for Psychical Study.

'The medium told us that the old lady is still up there in that room because she is quite happy. So there is no point in making her go against her will. So we still have one ghost—ironically enough, the one we once knew nothing about. She still bangs on the wall and moves the furniture, but as she is quite happy we will leave her.'

Miss Wright added a postscript; 'I almost forgot to mention that last night the old lady was banging on the wall and I am wondering if perhaps she is trying to get in touch with us?'

Ghosts from the Blitz?

89 KING'S ARMS, Peckham Rye, S.E.15.
A Courage house, south of the Thames at No. 132 Peckham Rye. Open: 11 to 3 & 5.30 to 11. Sunday: 12 to 2 & 7 to 10.30. Snacks and lunches. London Transport buses Nos. 12, 63 and 78 pass the door. Nearest station: Peckham (Southern Region). Telephone: 639/4085 and 4149.

GERMAN BOMBERS over London in 1940 scored a direct hit on the old King's Arms. It was a night of terror Peckham Rye finds it hard to forget, when the bodies of a good many regulars were clawed from the debris of the wrecked pub, some injured, eleven dead. Since then there have been paranormal occurrences which suggest that the new pub, rebuilt on the site of the old, is haunted. 'There is definitely something peculiar,' said a barmaid. 'I don't think it's a ghost. More like a poltergeist.' The landlord (of 1968) and his wife, Mr and Mrs Anthony King, recall various instances of inexplicable footsteps and strange noises at night, of objects being moved and the hysterical behaviour of their dog for no apparent reason. 'We were not believers in the supernatural at first,' said Mrs King, 'but this sort of thing makes you think.'

'The Thing' on the Stairs

90 OLD QUEEN'S HEAD, Islington, N.1.
A Watney house in the Essex road, a short walk from The Angel. Open: 11 to 3 & 5.30 to 11. Saturday 7 to 11. Sunday: 12 to 2 & 7 to 10.30. Snacks at the bar. No parking or accommodation. London Transport buses Nos. 73, 38, 171 and 277 pass the door. Nearest station: The Angel (underground). Telephone: 359/2830.

ONE OF THE perks Sir Walter Raleigh received as a favourite of Queen Bess was the authority 'to make lycences for the keeping of taverns and retayling of wynes throughout England.' This is one of the pubs he licensed, which is not surprising, since it is said that he had the house built in the first place. It is curious all the same that if he was responsible for its building he never lived here, preferring to live near by at the Pied Bull Inn.

The Old Queen's Head, Islington (No. 90)

An old print of the Old Queen's Head, Islington (No. 90)

Other of the Queen's ministers and servants who considered Islington handy for commuting to and from Court found the place suited them. Lord Burleigh, the Lord Treasurer, was one. Thomas Cure, the Royal Saddler, another. The Earl of Essex lived here for a time and consequently the Queen herself made it an occasional stopping place.

When the old place was pulled down in 1829 and rebuilt, the massive Tudor fireplace was given house room in the new pub, so perhaps the ghost is one of the Elizabethan V.I.Ps who survived the demolition. Since, by all accounts it is the ghost of a woman that haunts the Olde Queen's Head, it may well be the shade of Queen Bess herself. Or is the landlord's wife right in thinking it may be the ghost of a little girl?

'Many, many times I have gone upstairs to our flat and the ghost has run upstairs in front of me,' says Mrs Arthur Potter. 'I have heard her feet tap-tapping up the stairs and along the passage, and I've heard the swish and rustle of her long dress as she moves.

'So has my daughter. One day I was working upstairs ironing, and I heard somebody coming along the passage. I called out: "Who's that?" My daughter answered from the next room, "I thought it was you, Mum." But it was the ghost. Since then I have heard it many times, usually in the late afternoon, though I have never seen anything.'

Going downstairs one morning Mr Potter collided with the ghost. 'The light switch at the top of the stairs would not work when I flicked it on,' says Mr Potter, 'so the stairs were in darkness as I went down for the first time one morning. About half way down I felt this body, this thing, come against me. I pushed it away and rushed down the rest of the stairs. I practically fell down them to get to the light switch at the bottom. Don't ask me what it was. I don't know, but I just couldn't get down those stairs fast enough.'

Dick Turpin's Hide-out

91   THE SPANIARDS, Hampstead Heath, N.6.
*A Bass Charrington house on the Heath. Open : 11 to 3 & 5.30 to 11.
Sunday : 12 to 2 & 7 to 10.30. Snacks. Parking. Nearest station :
Hampstead (underground). London Transport buses pass door.
Telephone : 455/3276.*

DICK TURPIN left a number of ghosts behind him, most of them riding a phantom Black Bess. He is reported to have been seen a dozen times or more on Hampstead Heath, galloping towards The Spaniards Inn, which he used as a headquarters at the London end of the York road. Leading from the cellar of The Spaniards are secret passages which Turpin used to dodge the Bow Street runners. Many a landlord of The Spaniards has heard the sound of horses' hoofbeats—and found nothing material to account for them.

However, there are a number of very material relics of Turpin's existence still to be seen at this pub: pistols, keys, the knives and forks

'I give you three years—then hang!', said a witch to Dick
Turpin. He probably thought it over in The Spaniards . . .

he was using when arrested, the leg-irons that confined him before his execution. Look too at the little window in the staircase; it was made so that food could be passed to him in hiding.

No one knows how The Spaniards got its name. It may be from the Spanish Armada, for the house is said to have been built in the same year, or because the Spanish Ambassador to James I stayed there. Or the name may come from two Spanish brothers who were landlords of the inn and who fought a duel over a girl, with fatal consequences to one of them.

Or is G J Monson-Fitzjohn nearer the mark in his book, *Quaint Signs of Olde Inns*? He says: 'This house, before becoming a house of refreshment, was for many years used as the Spanish Embassy. The darkcomplexioned Spaniards so impressed themselves on the minds of the natives of Hampstead that the latter wrote weird things in their diaries about them, and caused the house to be known always as The Spaniards' (House).'

The Spaniards Inn, Hampstead Heath (No. 91) in 1899

Norfolk

The Ravished Maiden

92   OLD FERRY INN, Horning.
A Watney Mann house, about a mile south of Horning on the B1354. Open: 10 to 2.30 & 6 to 10.30. Friday and Saturday to 11. Sundays: 12 to 2 & 7 to 10.30. Snacks at bar. Lunch and dinner. Accommodation: 7 rooms. Nearest station: Wroxham. Telephone: Horning 259.

ANYBODY WHO messes about in boats knows Horning, on the winding River Bure. It is one of the most popular yachting centres on the Norfolk Broads. In the height of summer the river is alive with sail and come September, craft big and small gather there for a week-long regatta. And in September—but only once in every twenty years—crowds gather in the hope of seeing Horning's ghost.

About a mile downstream from the village is the Old Ferry Inn, which centuries ago was a mead house used by the local monks to stock up their cellars with enough of the heady brew to last them through a cheerless East Anglian winter. Here, late one summer's day, a young and lovely local girl was seized by the monks in a fit of drunken passion. They raped and murdered her and flung her body into the river.

One of her reappearances was on September 25, 1936, when the pub's licensee of that time reported: 'I was awaiting the return of a resident. It was about midnight. I was dozing. Then suddenly I was wide awake. I heard a noise, a rustling. Not three yards from me, in the passage leading to the staircase, was the frail shadowy form of a girl of about 25. She wore a greenish grey cloak, but it was her face that most attracted my attention. It was beautiful yet deathly white and had a look of suffering.

'I spoke to her and went towards her, but she glided in front of me towards the door. She appeared to go through the door. I opened it and followed and was just in time to see her disappear at the edge of the river near the chain ferry.'

A resident at the inn, sitting outside smoking a last cigarette before bed, vouched for the apparition. 'I heard the landlord cry out,' he said: 'The next moment the slim figure of this girl glided past me into the water; but I did not see her face.'

(Reprinted from *The Ghost Tour*, Wolfe Publishing).

The Goat's Head

93 GOAT INN, Strumpshaw, near Brundall.
*A Watney Mann house, 1½ miles south of A47, the Norwich to
Yarmouth road. Open : 10.30 to 2.30 & 6 to 11. Serves food. Parking.
Nearest station : Lingwood. Telephone : Brundall 3176.*

A GOAT'S HEAD, which used to hang on the wall of this 400-year-old
inn, has been taken down and locked in the woodshed. The landlord
believes that the head—which symbolises the Devil—could be the
cause of the hauntings at the pub. His wife and daughter say they have
seen ghostly shapes in the night, and that mirrors have fallen from the
wall, a piano has played by itself and the jukebox makes music without
a record on the turntable.

One of the most curious things that has happened is the dripping
of water from the beamed ceiling over the bar, though the tiled roof is
in sound repair. This happens when least expected and never causes
an electrical short-circuit in spite of water running down the bulb
holders and dripping off the bulb.

A medium who was invited to investigate these occurrences said the
haunting was by somebody who had been in the Navy and was surrounded by water. This has caused the landlord and his wife to suspect
it may be the ghost of a relative killed on the destroyer *Harvester*, sunk
during World War II.

Northamptonshire

The Ghost the King Saw

94 THE WHEATSHEAF, Daventry.
*A Watney Mann house in Sheaf Street. Open: 10 to 2 & 5.30 to
10.30. Sundays: 12 to 2 & 7 to 10.30. Snacks, lunch and dinner.
Parking. Accommodation. Nearest station: Northampton (12 mls.).
Telephone: Daventry 2515.*

KING CHARLES I seems to be the only person to have seen a ghost
at this inn, a solo haunting that has gone down in many of the history
books. The King stayed here for several nights before fighting the
Battle of Naseby, where he was routed and the Royalist cause shattered. Perhaps if he had heeded the warning he was given by the ghost
he saw he may not have lost all to Cromwell and his new model army.

The night before the battle the King had been in bed for about two
hours when the guard outside his room heard an unusual noise and
went in to see if anything was wrong. He found the King sitting up in
bed, looking alarmed. The King said he had seen a ghost, which he
knew to be the ghost of Lord Strafford, to whom he had given an under-
taking that not a hair of his head should be harmed and then consented
to his execution.

Strafford's enraged ghost said he had come to return good for evil
and warned the King not to fight the Parliamentary Army as he could
never win the day.

After that Charles slept fitfully. He was agitated by the warning and
in the morning was up early to consult with his nephew, Prince Rupert,
who pooh-poohed the whole thing as the nightmare of a conscience-
stricken man. So the King was persuaded not to call off the battle,
and the Royalists attacked on the morning of June 14, 1645. Prince
Rupert's Cavaliers met with instant success, but the King's forces were
defeated and scattered into the Northamptonshire hills. Many times
afterwards, while on the run, dejected King Charles was heard to say
that he wished he had taken the ghostly advice given to him that night
at The Wheatsheaf.

Charles was a care-free lad of 12 when this inn was built. Since then
it has been modernised many times. The bedroom in which the King
saw the ghost has been divided into two and a fine old fireplace and

some delightful panelling removed, but without disturbing the ghost. Over the years there have been vague rumours of a haunting but nothing more.

The Phantom Monk

95 THE OLD JOLLY SMOKERS, Northampton.
A Phipps/Watney Mann house which stood at 25 The Mayorhold, in the old part of the city which is being extensively redeveloped. At the time of going to press we learn that the pub has been demolished and that a new hotel is being built on the site.

BELOW this pub was a maze of subterranean passages dug by the monks centuries ago to link two monasteries, which might have explained the ghostly cowled figure seen there from time to time and the smell of incense that drifted about the house late at night.

The Haunted Staircase

96 TALBOT HOTEL, Oundle, near Peterborough.
A John Smith's 'Acorn' hotel. Accommodation: 15 bedrooms. The hotel hours are 8 a.m. to midnight. Licensing hours: 10.30 to 2.30 & 6 to 10.30. Lunch and dinner. Parking. Nearest station: Peterborough. Telephone: Oundle 2523 & 3520.

THIS PLACE was an inn for 150 years before King Alfred burned the cakes while on the run in Somerset. When the Conqueror swept up the Pevensey beaches on D-Day 1066 it was known as the Tabret Inn and kept that name until an enterprising landlord named William Whitwell took it over in 1600. He was a man for improvement and progress, a man of business who seized every opportunity that came his way. When he heard that the King, James VI of Scotland, son of Mary Queen of Scots, had ordered that near-by Fotheringhay Castle was to be razed to the ground, he was quick to snap up a great proportion of the interior decorations and the great horn windows.

He also bought the oak stairway which led to the top rooms of Fotheringhay Castle where Mary had been kept under house arrest until her execution in 1587.

With the stairway he bought a ghost—Mary's ghost.

That stairway is still used in the Talbot. One part of it is divided by a small wicket gate, which marked the boundary of Mary's prison confines. She was never allowed beyond it. In the well-worn, polished wood of the balustrade is the outline of a crown. That, say local historians, was made by a ring on Mary's hand as she gripped the balustrade on her way to the block. That is for everyone to see and examine. Not so the ghost.

The Talbot Hotel, Oundle (No. 96)

The haunted staircase of the Talbot

Room 5 at the top of the Fotheringhay staircase is the place where it all happens. Guests in that room have often, completely independently, complained of suddenly feeling cold in the night. They have commented on strange noises which sound like a woman's footsteps walking along the corridor. Others talk of hearing a 'wailing noise, like a woman singing.'

On one anniversary of Mary's execution a guest sleeping in Room 6 reported hearing a woman loudly sobbing in the next room—which that night was empty. The time was seven in the morning; just an hour before Mary was led away to her execution.

One woman who has slept in Room 5 and who has worked at the Talbot for more than 35 years says: 'I was lying in bed when I felt something resting on the bedclothes. I thought it might be the dog, so I tried to put my hand out to switch on the light. But I could not move. It felt as though a clammy mist was pressing me down. I still do not believe in ghosts but I certainly would not sleep in that room again.

Nowadays Room 5 is not used very much. 'It's always the last one to go,' says the receptionist: 'We use it only when the hotel is completely full.'

There is one person who has come face to face with the ghost of the Talbot, and she is the cook who has worked there for more than 20 years. She recalls: 'I saw a woman standing in the entrance to the office, wearing a long, full, buff-coloured dress with a white blouse and what looked like a small cap and apron. I asked the head waiter who she was and he said there was nobody in the hotel that evening, apart from us two. I went straight back but she had vanished completely.'

The horn windows, which came from Fotheringhay and through which the Queen looked down on the preparations for her death, now look out on the courtyard of the Talbot. People crossing the yard say they have seen her ghost standing by the staircase window, gazing out defiantly as she did that grim morning in February 1587.

It is on record that the executioner who was to behead the Queen lodged at the Talbot the night before and 'partook of pigeon pie, drank a quart of best ale and made a merry discourse with the serving girl till an early hour of the morning.'

The luckless Mary meanwhile, spent a last tearful night, just four miles away, writing letters and praying.

● FEETNOTE: Over the door of a stable in the hotel courtyard hang the bones of a pair of human feet, their age estimated at about 200 years. How did they come to be there—and why? Nobody really knows. The most popular theory is that they are the bones of a man who was beheaded for some ghastly crime committed at the Talbot, and that the landlord of the day hung up the feet as a warning to anybody contemplating a similar crime.

The Tragic Queen

97 THE HAYCOCK HOTEL, Wansford.
A two-star hotel in the town centre. Open : 10 to 2 & 6 to 10 (Summer 10.30). Sunday : 12.30 to 2 & 7 to 10. Accommodation : 18 bedrooms. Lunch and dinner. Snacks at bar. Ample parking. Nearest station : Stamford. Telephone : Wansford 223.

WHEN THE FIFTH Viscount Torrington, that indefatigable traveller and literary man, stayed at The Haycock in 1790, he scribbled in his diary: 'I arrived here last night to a good supper and a good night's rest in the best of rooms, pleasantly situated; the bridge, the river, the church beyond and all about constitute the right inn scenery . . .'

Obviously he was well pleased with the place. So was Princess Victoria Alexandrine—later Queen Victoria—who, accompanied by her mother the Duchess of Kent, dined and slept here in 1835. She was so delighted with the accommodation that she gave the landlady a signed portrait of herself when she left.

Did Mary Queen of Scots enjoy her stay here? It is said she was put up at The Haycock by her custodian, Sir William FitzWilliam, on the way to imprisonment to Fotheringhay Castle. That was in 1586. A year later Mary lost her head, since when her ghost is said to have freely roamed the corridors and rooms of this massive but beautiful building.

Once quizzed about the haunting by a reporter from the *Peterborough Telegraph,* the landlord commented: 'If we do have a ghost it must be a very contented one because there is a very happy atmosphere and the ghost is quite welcome to stay.'

But how did such an imposing mansion get such a unique name? Quite simply this: There was a time when Haycock ale brewed in the small alehouse in the yard behind the hotel's Jacobean frontage was drunk all over England. That was before Wansford was by-passed and the 13 arches of the old stone bridge carried the Great North Road across the River Nen right to the front door of The Haycock.

Haycock ale is good strong beer, which so overcame one country-man who slaked his thirst at the inn, that he went to sleep on a truss of hay by the side of the River Nen. While he slept the river flooded, carrying the truss of hay with its sleeping passenger downstream to the town bridge, which inspired the pub's name and prompted Taylor, the water poet, to pen these lines:

> On a haycock sleeping soundly,
> The river rose, and took me roundly
> Down the current; people cried,
> As along the stream I hied.
> 'Where away?' quoth they, 'from Greenland?'
> 'No; from Wansford Bridge in England.'

Northumberland

Dorothy's Ghost

98 LORD CREWE ARMS, Blanchland.
*A Swallow hotel of Vaux breweries, 12 miles south of Hexham on
B6306. Open: Hotel—24 hours service. Licensing hours: 11 to 3 &
6 to 10.30. Lunches and dinner. Accommodation: 14 bedrooms.
Parking. Nearest station: Hexham. Telephone: Blanchland 251.*

INDUSTRIAL Newcastle-upon-Tyne is only 30 miles from this delightful
but lonely place where the River Derwent tumbles down from the wild
Northumbrian moors into a tree-fringed valley, once the home of the
white-robed monks of Blanchland Abbey.

They began it all in 1165, so it is not surprising that one of the ghosts
that walks in the village is that of a red-haired monk, the victim of a
border raid by the Scots. Nobody in the village is in the least bit worried
by this ghost. They accept it as a matter of fact, as they do the ghost
of Dorothy Forster, who haunts the Lord Crewe Arms. Originally this
was the Abbot's lodging house which, after the dissolution of the
monasteries, became a manor house and then the home of the Forster
family, who were active supporters of the Jacobite cause.

Thomas Forster, anxious to see the Stuarts back on the throne,
plotted the rebellion of 1715 with his neighbour Lord Derwentwater,
thought by some to be the lover of Tom's sister Dorothy. Their rebellion
was short-lived, ending at Preston without a fight.

The Hanoverians beheaded the 27-year-old Earl of Derwentwater and
removed Forster to Newgate prison to await trial for high treason. But
his sister had other ideas. She rode to London pillion behind the
blacksmith from neighbouring Adderstone. With duplicate keys, plus
a large measure of ingenuity and courage, she outwitted the prison
governor and his guards to free her brother. According to one story
she took him back to Blanchland and hid him in a secret room behind
the kitchen chimney. Eventually he was smuggled to France.

The ghost which haunts the Lord Crewe is usually presumed to be
that of Tom's sister. She is thought to be seeking the help of those she
finds sleeping in what was once her bedroom, attempting perhaps to
get a message to her exiled brother. But there are those who dispute it,
saying it could be Dorothy Forster's aunt, who at 21 married Lord
Nathaniel Crewe, the 79-year-old Bishop of Durham. Her name was also

Dorothy Forster, and her portrait, attributed to Sir Peter Lely, hangs in the hotel dining-room. Her niece's portrait hangs in the sitting room which is named after her.

Whichever of these two equally lovely ladies is the ghost, there are countless people who claim to have seen her. Some years back the local vicar saw her walking across the village square, but only realised it was the ghost when he got no response to his 'Good evening.'

The man who was manager in the mid-sixties, Mr Gerry Coley, says that though he never encountered Dorothy's ghost there are plenty of people who have. 'They talk about her as if they knew her personally,' he said. 'I had one guest who booked in for three nights and after two checked out, saying he could not stand it any longer. He was disturbed both nights by something in his room.'

On the other hand there are people, scores of them, who have travelled half across the world hopeful of spending a disturbed night in the haunted wing of this fascinating inn. Mrs Hazel Jones and her husband Graham came from Ontario, Canada, to stay there on a wet night in 1966, an experience which she afterwards described in these words in the British Travel Association magazine *In Britain*:

'When we finally retired for the night the room across the hall looked benign and friendly enough, yet I debated whether to suggest that we leave the bedside lamp on. But there's no such thing as a ghost, I assured myself—and, cuddling the thought as if it were a teddy bear, I dropped off to sleep like a three-year-old.

'Hours later I partially awoke, oblivious as to where we were and only knowing that my shoulder and neck were in a draught. Then someone touched me . . . on the side away from Gray!

'I was awake, fully awake now. It was as if my eyes flew open but remained shut at the same time. And I wasn't dreaming. I was absolutely alert in every sense. I was conscious of Gray's heavy breathing. I never moved a muscle—lacking the courage even to open my eyes.

'Next thing I felt a thump at the bottom of the bed. I can only describe it as if a heavy cat had silently leapt up and tramped across our feet a few times looking for a place to settle—then decided to jump off. This was followed by a sensation of someone bumping the bed and gently shaking my feet, as one would in trying to rouse a heavy sleeper. I did the only thing that seemed sensible at the time. My knees shot up, my head shot down, and I curled up under the covers. The commotion stopped.

'Long minutes later, I slid slowly up and peered round. My eyes were open now but there was nothing to see. We hadn't drawn the curtains and I could easily make out the stone outline of the chapel window frame, as the faintest grey light tinted the sky. It was still raining. I lay there wide-eyed, searching for a reasonable explanation. None would come. There was no solution other than to say it had all been a dream. And yet—

'Then I heard it. A muffled knock at our door—urgent, secret. Four raps by a gloved hand. I sat bolt upright in bed. Gray propped himself up on his elbow, suddenly alert.

'Listen!' I whispered. The knocking came again, hurried, desperate. But this time it seemed to be on the wall side of our clothes cupboard. And then I sensed it. An elusive something—a memory perhaps—was moving slowly in the alcove to answer a door which had long since vanished. 'Someone's in the corner!' I choked out. Gray dived for the bedside lamp. It clicked on. The room was empty. The feeling of a presence was gone. My nylons drying on the towel rack jolted us back to normal.

'I *must* have been dreaming,' I said, as a feeling of foolishness began to replace the panic. 'It could have been a noise in the water pipes,' Gray added simply. The lamp stayed on.'

The Witches' Revenge

99 WELLINGTON HOTEL, Riding Mill.
A Scottish and Newcastle house on A68, three miles south of Corbridge. Open : 10.30 to 3 & 6 to 10.30. Sunday : 12 to 2 & 7 to 10. Snacks, lunches and dinner. Parking. Nearest station : Riding Mill. Telephone : Riding Mill 239 and 226.

THREE CENTURIES ago the witches of Newcastle-upon-Tyne used the little back room of what is now the Wellington Hotel to feast and practise their incantations. On the evidence of a servant girl named Anne Armstrong, a known witch-hunter, five of them were brought to trial at Morpeth Assizes in the summer of 1673. Presumably they escaped burning—or at least some of them did—since it appears they took their revenge on Anne. They caught her spying on their continued activities in the little back room. She was hanged there by a rope that often figured in their revels. It is her ghost that is thought to haunt Riding Mill—in particular the bedroom where she used to sleep between witch-hunts.

Oxfordshire

The Deserter

100 THE REINDEER, Banbury.

A Hook Norton house on Parson Street in the town centre. Open: 10 to 2.30 & 6 to 10.30. (Saturday to 11.) Sunday: 12 to 2 & 7 to 10.30. Snacks at bar. Nearest station: Banbury. Telephone: Banbury 29221.

THIS CLAIMS to be the oldest inn in Banbury sited in one of the town's oldest streets. You can't miss it because it has a sign which extends virtually right across the narrow thoroughfare. Inside there is a maze of small rooms and connecting passages which for years have been the haunt of 'a grim Cavalier figure.' It is thought that the Cavalier was one of those tried in the famous Globe Room at the Reindeer Inn when Oliver Cromwell held Parliament there. In recent years Banbury Council bought the original Globe Room panelling and its magnificent plaster ceiling for installation in the new Civic Centre. Comments Mrs Joy Oxlade, landlord's daughter: 'I have seen the ghost and so have my two children. They were terrified. But the ghost has not been about since they moved that panelling to the Town Hall.'

John Hampden's Haunt

101 THE PLOUGH, Clifton Hampden.

A Watney Mann house on A415, Abingdon to Burcot road, once the main road to Oxford. Open: 10.30 to 2.30 & 6.30 to 10. Sunday: 12 to 2 & 7 to 10.30. Accommodation. Snacks and lunch. Parking. Nearest station: Culham (2 mls.). Telephone: Clifton Hampden 311.

JOHN HAMPDEN'S ghost is thought to walk here. The village was part of the Hampden family estate in earlier times and there can be little doubt that this cousin of Oliver Cromwell, and active supporter of the Parliamentary Forces, looked in at The Plough whenever he came this way.

The room named after him was the parlour of the thatched and shuttered inn where, in the early summer of 1643, he rested between clashes with King Charles's army. Barely a five-mile ride is Chalgrove Field, the scene of an ill-fated skirmish with Prince Rupert's fiery cavalry. Six days later on June 24, John Hampden died of his wounds, a great loss to the Puritan cause.

The behaviour of the ghost at The Plough suggests that it too has puritanical leanings judging by its disapproval on one occasion of the landlady's choice of nightcap. The person who best remembers that incident—and others—is Mrs Heron Maund, who once ran this inn with her late husband and had a number of brushes with the ghost which left her wondering.

'Neither my husband nor I spoke about the presence for a long time,' said Mrs Maund.* 'Then one day my husband said to me: "When you are serving in the bar do you ever feel someone nudging you?"

'I replied that I often did and would turn round expecting to find him —my husband—behind me, but he was either not in the bar at all or too far away to have touched me. I had not mentioned it to him as I felt he would laugh at me.

'When we discovered the experience was mutual, he went on to tell me how often on a quiet winter's morning he would be doing something in the back kitchen when he would hear the bar-door latch go and come out to serve a customer only to find no one there—except sometimes a sort of blue light going through the closed door between the two bars. I laughed at this and said evidently the ghost wanted to get his beer cheaper by going through into the tap-room.

'But I ceased to laugh when one night after we had closed we were having a night-cap before retiring: my husband had given me a small glass of whisky and turned to get himself one. Neither of us was near the counter but suddenly my glass turned completely upside down and emptied the contents on to the counter. I would add that this was our only drink that evening so it was not the effect of alcohol!'

Mrs Maund talked also of the ghost of a pet collie dog killed on the road outside The Plough: 'I often felt him pushing his nose into my hand when I was in the bar,' she said. 'I said nothing to my husband as he was very upset over the death of the dog.

'But one day—just as in the other case—he asked me if I ever felt the dog's nose against my hand. He, like me, had experienced the dog's presence although the animal had been dead for some weeks.'

* Talking to Anthony Wood of *The Oxford Mail* in 1966.

The Maiden Forlorn

102 THE GEORGE, Dorchester-on-Thames.
A Morlands house on the main Henley to Oxford road (A425). Open: 10.30 to 2 & 6 to 10.30. Saturday: 11 o'clock. Sunday: 12 to 2 & 7 to 10. Lunches and dinners. Parking. Accommodation: 22 bedrooms. Nearest station: Didcot. Telephone: Warborough 281.

A THOUSAND YEARS ago there was an inn on this site, a hospice belonging to the Abbey of the cathedral city of Mercia, the Wessex capital. The city and its cathedral have gone, so has the monastery. But not the abbey; that is just across the way from The George. What was once the monks' brew house is now the hotel dining-room, with a raftered roof that would not look out of place in a cathedral.

Sarah, the first Duchess of Marlborough, made The George her overnight stopping place when coaching from Woodstock to St James's. She slept as guests do today, in the 'travellers lodgings,' the original half-timbered rooms leading off a surrounding gallery, reached by a staircase from the inn yard. One of these rooms, named 'The Vicar's Room,' is haunted by the ghost of a sad looking young girl in a white gown. She was last seen in 1968.

Those who have experienced this haunting say she stands at the foot of the large canopied four-poster bed, then turns forlornly away to fade from sight.

The Friendly Ghost

103 LANGSTONE ARMS HOTEL, Kingham.
A free house off B4450, the Stow-on-the-Wold to Chipping Norton road Open: 10.30 to 2.30 & 6 to 10. Sunday: 12 to 2 & 7 to 10.30. Snacks at the bar. Parking. Nearest station: Kingham. Telephone: Kingham 209.

'EXORCISM is for evil ghosts and I am convinced this one is not evil.' That was the opinion of the Rev. Harry Cheales, a Church of England expert on ghosts, after he had spent some time at the Langstone Arms investigating the 'faintly-luminous Victorian female who has haunted the hotel corridors by night or day for years.'

'When I visited the hotel and said a few prayers, this ghost became quite peaceful,' commented Mr Cheales, and added: 'The friendly ones must be left alone. You can get into a nasty mess if you attempt to exorcise a friendly ghost. I found this out a few years ago when one got its own back by throwing me out of bed.'

So far there have been no reports of the Langstone ghost doing anything more violent than manifesting itself as a 'whitish shape,' about 5 ft. 3 in. tall, usually heralded by the sound of coughing from an empty room.

The pub's regulars have seen the apparition gliding along behind the bar and passing effortlessly through a piece of mahogany furniture. Some say the shape is that of a woman, others that it is faintly luminous. None could discern any features, but one thought it had a headdress similar to that worn by a nun.

The possibility of this ghost being that of a nun is an unlikely one; the Langstone was originally built, slightly pre-Victorian, as a hunting lodge for the local squire.

The Uneasy Bed

104 THE BIRD CAGE, Thame.

A Courage house in the market place. Open : 10 to 2.30 & 6 to 10.30. (Saturday to 11.) Sunday : 12 to 2 & 7 to 10.30. Snacks. Accommodation : 3 bedrooms. Street parking. Nearest station : Thame. Telephone : Thame 46.

A PICTURESQUE pub with a picturesque name acquired during the Napoleonic wars. In those days it was The Blackbird but was very quickly dubbed The Bird and Cage when French soldiers were imprisoned in the cellars. How it came to be haunted is a mystery. In the dark hours between 2.30 and 3 tired-sounding footsteps are heard, followed by a gentle tapping on bedroom doors. The footsteps always follow the same route from a first floor bedroom, up the narrow, twisted stairs, to two bedrooms at the top of the house. In one of the rooms is a bed in which guests find it impossible to sleep undisturbed.

Father Dominique

105 THE CROWN, Pishill.

A free house on the road between Henley and Watlington (B480). Open : 10 to 2.30 & 6 to 10.30 (except Monday). Saturday, open to 11. No accommodation. Luncheon and dinner. The barn adjoining is a licensed club open Wednesday to Saturday, 8.30 to 2 a.m. Ample parking. Nearest station : Henley-on Thames. Telephone : Turville Heath 364.

IT IS PUBS such as this that make the countryside of the Chilterns so more-ish. All those things that are said about it in the guide books are true. It IS interesting, it IS charming, it IS picturesque, and it is absolutely breathtaking in the summer when the wisteria is blooming and engulfing it from roof to road in a cascade of mauve. The 16th-century thatched barn at the end of the garden is equally as lovely with giant hollyhocks and great plumes of roses growing against its weather-boarded walls.

In the 11th century there was a farm house on this site, replaced in Tudor times by the present building, which during the Reformation gave sanctuary to many a Jesuit priest. One, Father Dominique, strayed long enough from his upstairs hiding place to meet a girl named Elizabeth lodging at the inn. They fell in love and met more and more frequently. Once, when they were together in the garden, Elizabeth buried a gold piece in the shadow of the stable wall saying it was a token of her love. The priest, overwhelmed by this impulsive act of affection, pledged that he would gladly die for her. A few days later he did, fighting a duel to defend her name.

His body lies in the near-by church yard and his ghost still haunts The Crown. It is seen at times, usually quite late at night, sitting in a

The Crown, Pishill (No. 105)

corner of the bar, wearing a black cloak and a wide-brimmed hat.

'I have heard it in the evenings walking along the passage upstairs,' says Mrs Patrick King, the wife of the proprietor. 'One can hear the footsteps quite plainly.'

WHAT'S IN A NAME-NOTE: How The Crown got its name I know not, but I am assured the village was so called after the regular habits of the stage coach drivers who stopped here at the end of the long pull up from Watlington.

Sad, Mad Maude

106 WESTON MANOR HOTEL, Weston-on-the-Green.
A three star hotel on A43, the Oxford to Northampton road. Bars open: 10.30 to 2.30 & 6 to 10. Sunday: 12 to 2 & 7 to 10.30. Lunches and dinner. Accommodation: 18 beds, 7 with bath. Parking. Nearest station: Bicester North. Telephone: Bletchington 260 and 330.

MAD MAUDE was a nun burned at the stake for her immoral behaviour at the manor in the days when it was a monastery. She haunts the oak bedroom, which presumably is where this favourite of the brothers transgressed once too often, to end her days shrieking for mercy as the flames leapt around her.

An equally dramatic haunting but one not so often witnessed at the Weston Manor is that of the ghostly coach and horses seen at night careering through the rear courtyard of the old stables. A number of visitors occupying bedrooms overlooking the courtyard have heard the ghost coach; fewer have seen it, though there is one elderly villager who has both seen and heard it and refuses to walk in the yard after dark.

Shropshire

The Old Soldier

107 THE GLOBE, Ludlow.
A Wrekin house in Market Street in town centre. Open : 10 to 2.30
& 6 to 10.30. Sunday : 12 to 2 & 7 to 10.30. Snacks. Accommodation.
Parking. Nearest station : Ludlow. Telephone : Ludlow 2709.

THE GLOBE is in the oldest quarter of Ludlow, within a hundred yards of the ruined Norman castle. Perhaps it is not as lovely to look at as its black-and-white timbered rival, The Feathers, but it is as old— and, what's more, it is haunted. The ghost is of a bewigged man, who wears a cloak about his shoulders. He is thought to be Edward Dobsod, a soldier murdered at The Globe while garrisoned at Ludlow in 1553. A Birmingham business man, on the landing of the hotel's second floor at two in the morning, saw a figure approaching and stood aside to let it pass. He received no reply to his greeting and next day discovered he'd said goodnight to the ghost.

Somerset

The Laughing Gambler

108 GARRICKS HEAD HOTEL, Bath.
A Courage house in the Shaw Close in city centre. Open: 10.30 to 2.30 & 5.30 to 10.30 (Saturday: 11). Sunday: 12 to 2 & 7 to 10.30. Bed and breakfast. Nearest station: Bath Spa. Telephone: Bath 0225/25060.

IN THE 18th century the old Garricks Head was a gambling den, run by Beau Nash. It is next door to the Theatre Royal and was once connected by secret passage to give the young bucks a quick retreat when things were not going their way. It must have seen many a clash of steel in settlement of a wager, many a duel over a woman's love. And as a result it seems to have a couple of ghosts to its credit.

One for sure is a heavily-built man with a long brown wig which touches the shoulders of his Regency costume. He's been both seen and heard, once by the son of a former landlord, who saw him entering the secret passage. True to ghostly form, he leaves no footprints though he has been heard moving about with squeaky footfalls. Down in the cellar there is sometimes a strong smell of perfume. This could, of course, belong to the same ghost, or it could be the ghost of a woman who hanged herself behind a bedroom door because the man she loved lost a duel in which she was the prize.

Then there's the grey lady from the neighbouring theatre who committed suicide by throwing herself from the window of a room above the bar. She has been seen from the stage of the Theatre Royal many times, sitting in a box watching the performance. Once she was blamed because a grandfather clock chimed in the middle of a scene, when it should have kept silent. Apart from that unsporting gesture, these are all friendly ghosts.

Since I told that story in *The Ghost Tour* (1967) the Garricks Head has again changed its landlord. Tradition has it that a ghost always becomes more active whenever a new landlord takes over.

When Robert Simmons of the *Bristol Evening Post* went to see him this is what he said:

'The first day here my keys vanished. Then they turned up in the middle of the lounge floor. It is a large bunch of keys and quite impossible for them to have been there all the time.

'I am not a fanciful man, but every time I go down into the cellars I can feel something, a sort of presence. It's spine-chilling.

'I don't mind having a ghost in the house but the tricks he plays are annoying. He stole the mallet with which I drive bungs into barrels, literally from behind my back. It weighs several pounds but just disappeared into thin air. It was several days before I found it again.'

Said the wife of the landlord, 'I do not really believe in such things as ghosts, but such odd things happen in this place. There are noises on the stairs and noises in the attic no one can explain.

'Since we have been here my baby has been waking every morning at 3 am. Something disturbs her. She does not cry, but grumbles to herself for 20 minutes and then goes to sleep again.'

An 18-year-old repertory actress staying at the Garricks Head at about this time reported that late on her first night in the hotel, someone knocked on her bedroom door. She called 'come in,' and the door handle began to turn. But there was no one there. 'It was really scary,' she said. 'I was with another girl and we were both terrified.'

A rumbling ghostly laugh woke her and other guests at 3 am one morning. 'We were all sleeping in different rooms and we all woke and went into the passage to listen. There was nothing imaginary about it,' she commented.

On another occasion she woke to find her room 'filled with a strange glow.' When she snapped on the light it disappeared.

The Nun Looks In

109 BLUE ANCHOR, Cannington.
A Whitbread house on A39, the Bridgewater to Minehead road. Open: 10 to 2.30 & 6 to 10.30. Sunday: 12 to 2 & 7 to 10.30. Accommodation. Serves food. Nearest station: Bridgewater. Telephone: Combwich 215.

A FEW STEPS along the road from this pub is the Somerset Farm Institute, which was once a nunnery, home of a community of 12 Benedictine sisters and a prioress.

Three of the nuns transgressed and were so severely beaten for their transgression that one of them died. She, say the villagers, is the nun whose ghost looks in at the Blue Anchor. She has been seen walking in an upstairs corridor of the inn, and crossing the little bridge over the brook which runs near by.

Says the wife of the licensee: 'I have seen her many times, but every time I try to talk to her she disappears. She doesn't frighten me.'

Laughter in the Next Room

110 CHOUGHS HOTEL, Chard.

A Dutton's house in the town centre. Open : 10 to 2.30 & 6 to 10.30.
Friday and Saturday : to 11. Sunday : 12 to 2 & 7 to 10.30. Meals
and snacks. Accommodation. Parking. Nearest station : Axminster
(7 mls.). Telephone : Chard 3266.

BLOODY JUDGE JEFFREYS left his mark on the ancient town o
Chard and on Choughs. When he set up his Assize Court of roug
justice, Chard paid dearly for supporting Monmouth's rebels agains
James II. Jeffreys ordered that 12 men should be rounded up an
hanged from a great oak in the lower part of the town. One tree, whic
became known as 'Hangcross Oak,' was there until a few years ago
perpetuating the wretched memory of the unjust judge who lodged a
Choughs and whose ghost walks in a derelict upper room.

You may not see the ghost but you can certainly see the remains o
his lordship's coat of arms fashioned in the ceiling plaster of one o
the bedrooms, presumably that in which he slept. And there is
skeleton in a cupboard of this fine old gabled inn, a skeleton thre
centuries old, preserved under the terms of the lease. These moulderin
bones are those of the chough, a west country crow, after which th
inn is named.

The Unforgettable Moment

All of which in no way accounts for the strange things that happene
to Mrs Doreen Jones of Chalfont St Giles, when she stayed at this pu
in the years before World War II. In 1965 she told her story of th
moment she would never forget, to the *Daily Sketch*. This is he
experience:

'On that August Monday evening the heat was stifling. We ha
knocked on doors marked "Bed and Breakfast" from early afternoo
but there were no empty rooms anywhere. My friend had been feelin
ill all day and longed for somewhere to lie down.

'We were getting desperate as night approached. Hot, dusty an
tired, we came to the little town of Chard in Somerset, and went int
the first place we saw—the Choughs inn.

'We were in luck—there was room at the inn. My friend tottere
thankfully to her room at the back of the house. I went to my room ove
looking the street, and never did a bed seem more delightful.

'Sleepily I heard the landlord and his wife pass my door on their wa
to bed. Then all was silent and I fell asleep. Suddenly I was wide awak
I could hear voices, whispering and soft laughter. I got up and listene
at the door, then gently opened it and peered out. Not a soul was i
sight. All was silent in the sleeping house.

'As soon as I got back into bed the voices began again. Soft women
voices, whispering gently and laughing. Then a more forceful voic
with more than a hint of malice in it.

'This time I went to the window and looked out to see if there wa

nyone in the street. It was deserted. There wasn't even a light in any
f the windows near by. I went back to bed and lay perfectly still. Once
1ore the light, muffled sound of female voices came unmistakably to
1y ears.

'The more forceful voice seemed to be gaining ascendancy over the
thers, and a note of menace crept in. I could stand it no longer. I tore
ut of the room and took refuge with my friend at the other side of the
ouse.

'Next morning the landlady seemed in no mood to talk. She served
ur breakfast quickly and disappeared into the back premises. But on
!aving I did ask if there had been a party the night before. She eyed
1e very oddly and said there had been no one in the house but
urselves.

'Years later my husband and I were on holiday in the neighbourhood.
felt I had to call at the Choughs to find out if the atmosphere still
ffected me. The inn had passed into other hands, and over a glass
f the local cider I told the landlord of my experience.

'He told me of guests who had had similar experiences. One man
rho slept in "my room" dashed downstairs at first light with his
aggage and departed with all speed. Across his face was a red weal
s if inflicted by a riding whip—a sensation he had had during his
visitation." He too had heard female voices and laughter.

'His was not the only case. But the landlord wasn't anxious to talk
bout these things—he thought they were bad for trade. I told him I
hould have thought the reverse was true. He then disclosed that a
1eeting of the Psychical Research Society had been held there after
ll these reports of hauntings.

'Then he told me of the really interesting part. The inn had recently
een modernised. And what apparently was a solid wall at the head
f the bed was found, to everyone's astonishment, to be a dividing
rall. Between it and the wall of the next room a small chamber was
ound. Historians said it had been a ladies' powder room.

he Grudge From The Grave

'I have always longed to delve further into the history of the Choughs
1n—and even to stay in the same room again. According to the land-
rd, though, there were no more hauntings after the wall was knocked
own. One day I intend to make a sentimental pilgrimage and find out
ll I can about the experience I remember vividly to this day.

'Who in the past held a grudge so strong that it was carried beyond
1e grave? What happened there long ago? I would love to know.'

In response to a letter published in a local Devon newspaper, I found
1e widow of a previous landlord of the Choughs living at Ilfracombe.
he and her husband ran the hotel before the war. She does not recall
trange female voices at the dead of night, or the discovery of a secret
2om. Here is her story of a face-to-face encounter with the ghostly
gure of a man in armour.

'It was carnival night in Chard and we were busy at the hotel, so busy
1at we ran out of change. I told my husband that I would go up to the

bedroom and get some. This was about 9 o'clock. I took a torch and went upstairs. On my way back, at the door of the bedroom, I met this figure in armour, with chains on his wrists and ankles. I said, "Please let me pass," and the ghost disappeared in an instant.

'When I got back to the bar I didn't say anything to anybody. I kept it to myself until we closed and then told my husband what I had seen. It is something I'll never forget.'

Charlie the Skittler

111 HOLMAN CLAVEL INN, Culmhead, near Taunton.
A Whitbread house approached by way of A303 Ilminster to Honiton road. Open: 10.30 to 2 & 6 to 10.30. Snacks at bar. Accommodation (4 double, one single). Ample parking. Nearest station: Taunton. Telephone: Blagdon Hill 432.

BEHIND THIS little whitewashed stone pub, with its low-beamed ceilings, is a skittle alley. The inn itself is about 600 years old, having first been a resthouse for monks and later a bailiff's cottage. The skittle alley is a much later addition, built long after the bailiff had gone and the innkeeper was doing enough business to find the finance for a new line in healthy entertainment.

It is still used today, even by 'Charlie' as the ghost of the Holman Clavel is known by the villagers. They think little of it when they hear the wooden skittle balls thrown by some phantom hand, scattering the pins in the small hours.

Visitors stopping at the inn, knowing nothing of this extraordinary phenomena have awakened to hear the skittles in use in the early hours of the morning, long after the landlord has gone to bed. And all this in a skittle alley that is securely locked and bolted at closing time.

Not that being locked in for the night inhibits Charlie. Once his padding footsteps were heard in the passage leading to the bathroom. The son of the licensee of that time was in the bathroom and watched dumbstruck as he saw the door handle turn, heard the footsteps enter and move around the room. He felt the unseen presence too, and minutes later heard it go out, closing the door and padding back along the passage. He was a colonial policeman at that time, home on leave. The experience left him shocked and shaken.

His father reported another experience. 'It was exactly as if something had been pushed—a heavy piece of furniture like a wardrobe being pushed over. I went upstairs expecting to find something out of place but there was nothing. In these old places you sometimes get masonry falling, but it definitely wasn't masonry. And that was before the breaking of the sound barrier so it couldn't have been that.'

The present licensee remarks: 'Charlie is reputed to have been a monk who was unfrocked. Only one person has seen him, but many of my guests have felt his presence. Things keep disappearing—a key a postal order, stamps, little things. When we have forgotten about them they reappear.

'When we had the old-fashioned barrels we used to find pints of beer drawn overnight. We've heard some terrific crashes in the night and have come down expecting to find glass everywhere. But nothing. Everything is completely in order.'

The Fat Monk

112 GEORGE AND PILGRIM INN, High Street, Glastonbury.
A Hunt Edmunds hotel (Bass Charrington) in the town centre. Open: 10 to 2.30 & 6 to 10.30. Serves food as well as drink. Accommodation (12 bedrooms). Parking. Nearest station: Bridgwater Telephone: Glastonbury 3139.

THIS WAS the pilgrims' hotel of its day. Abbot John de Selwood had it built between 1470 and 1475 to cater for the 15th-century tourist trade to Glastonbury, pilgrims and others visiting the Abbey.

It stands at 18th in the Thomas Burke table of the oldest inns in England. At one time its interior decor was a hundred per cent austerity; visitors slept in individual cells and ate communally in a refectory.

One of the bedrooms which was formerly a cell is still visited by the ghostly presence of a fat and cheerful monk, with a hankering for 20th-century comfort.

If you find this inn's freestone exterior unusual you'll be equally impressed with the interior, with its stone stairway leading up from the stone hall and the surrounding snuggeries which look for all the world like chapels on loan from a cathedral.

The Spectral Guardian

113 THE PLOUGH, Holford.
A Whitbread house on A39 between Bridgwater and Minehead. Open: 10 to 2 & 5.30 to 11. Serves snacks. Limited accommodation. Ample parking. Nearest station: Bridgwater. Telephone: Holford 232.

COLERIDGE AND WORDSWORTH patronised this pub. Much more recently James Wentworth Day, the author, stopped here and afterwards wrote in *In Search of Ghosts*:

'You may hear from your bedroom window, set in stone walls as thick as a fort, the roaring of red stags, the grunt of the badger on his midnight rounds, the sharp yap of a hunting vixen or the startled cry of a heron as it rises from the trout stream which splashes down to the water-mill.'

Despite all that he slept well and wasn't disturbed by the ghost, a murdered Spanish merchant who put up at the inn one night in 1535 while on his way to Bristol. Before the Spaniard went to bed the affable regulars plied him with liquor to loosen his tongue. He found himself surrounded by jolly fellows who drank heartily in the glow of the fire, who talked a lot and invited him to do likewise in their anxiety to discover if he had money enough to make robbing him worth their while.

He had money enough and, suspecting the motives for their generosity, he hid it the moment he was alone in his bedroom. When the plotters crept in on him, he was stretched out on the bed snoring loudly. Beside him on the floor was an empty money bag. Enraged at being cheated of the money by his foreign cunning, his would-be robbers stabbed him to death as he slept. It is said in Holford that the money remains to this day where the Spaniard hid it, and that his ghost remains to keep a spectral eye upon it.

The Lady in White

114 COACH HOUSE, Locking.
A Whitbread house, off the A371, Axbridge-to-Weston road. Open: 10 to 2 & 6 to 10.30. Sunday: 12 to 2 & 7 to 10.30. Snacks at the bar. Lunch and dinner. Nearest station: Weston-super-Mare. Telephone: Banwell 24.

IN LOCKING'S pseudo Coach House, Sir John Plumley is just a name on a door. 'Plumley's Bar' it reads, and nine out of ten intent on downing their first pint of the day don't give poor old Sir John another thought.

Why should they? He lived a long time ago and if he hadn't made the simple mistake of backing a loser he would have been ignored by the historians, though he may still have had his name on a pub door, since this one is built in what used to be his backgarden. It was in fact, his coachhouse and stables.

Sir John was Lord of the Manor of Locking, with a wife and two sons. The locals used to tug their forelocks and call him sir, signs of respect that nowadays are music-hall jokes.

On that summer day in 1685 when James, Duke of Monmouth, the bastard son of King Charles II, landed at Lyme Regis, the peasants seized their pitchforks and rallied to his cause. Not so the gentry; most of them saw it as a foolish escapade and stayed at home. There were a few that didn't. One was Sir John, who with his two sons and a crocodile of able-bodied farmhands rode off to join Monmouth at Bridgwater. The remnants of Monmouth's routed forces after the battle at Sedgemoor took to the Mendips, Sir John among them. But not his sons. They, along with hundreds of others trying to escape into the Polden Hills, were trapped in the marshes and butchered.

Such a slaughter left an army of ghosts, among them a phantom cavalier horseman described in detail by those who consider it to be Monmouth himself.

He, though, is not the ghost of the Coach House. Neither, for that matter, is Sir John, who, after escaping, hid for a time in the Somerset countryside. Then, according to Francis Knight in his book *Sea-board of Mendip*, published in 1902, 'he returned after a while to his native village, and was hiding in the little wood still known as Plumley's Copse —though scant traces of it are now left south-east of Locking Head Farm—when the attention of a party of soldiers, who were quartered at the farm, and who were engaged in searching for rebels, and no doubt for John Plumley in particular, was attracted to the spot where he was concealed by the barking of his favourite dog.

It is said that he was dragged from his hiding-place behind a large stone, which still marks the spot, and hanged on a great elm hard by, about a hundred yards from the knoll called Garberry, close to Locking Head. The tree is still pointed out, but it was struck by lightning a few years ago and burned for two days.

'Overwhelmed with horror and despair, the unfortunate man's widow threw herself and the dog who, through his devotion to his master, had been the innocent cause of the catastrophe, down one of the wells in the garden, and the story was long current in the village that the figure of a lady in white, carrying a dog in her arms, was sometimes seen in the twilight gliding down the Ghost's Walk, at the back of the manor house, and vanishing between two yew trees by the mouth of a long disused well.'

The Judge and the Fiddler

115 THE CASTLE, Castle Green, Taunton.
A three-star hotel in the town centre. AA and RAC listed. Licensing hours: 10.30 to 2 & 6 to 10.30. Sunday: 12 to 2 & 7 to 10. Accommodation: 52 bedrooms. Dining-room open to non-residents. Parking. Nearest station: Taunton. Telephone: Taunton 2671.

THE CASTLE at Taunton is the real thing. It is not just another name for a pink-washed cottage huddled under the sandstone battlements. Much of the original Norman fortress was demolished after the Monmouth Rebellion in 1685 but what was left has been skilfully converted into a comfortable, modern hotel, with a not-so-modern ghost.

On the boisterous night of June 20 after the Duke of Monmouth had been proclaimed King from the Cross in Taunton's market place, officers of his rebel army celebrated at the Castle inn. They had been carousing lavishly since the previous day when a gaggle of lusty Somerset wenches had welcomed them with open arms.

The Bloody Assize that followed Monmouth's defeat was presided over by Judge Jeffreys in the same Great Hall of the Castle, where only weeks before all had been gaiety. The infamous Judge sentenced 200 Taunton men to be hanged, drawn and quartered, 800 to be sold into slavery, and those women of the town who gave a welcome to the Duke and his men, to be publicly flogged.

Small wonder a ghost walks. But whose ghost? Dip into Mr Wentworth Day's book *In Search of Ghosts* in which he refers to a night spent at The Castle: 'When at the tail-end of 1968 I cast-up at this attractive old hotel I was told I could sleep, if I wished, in the Royal Room. A chamber which has been occupied by various members of the Royal Family from time to time. In all, seven members of the British Royal Family and a former Queen of Portugal have stayed at the hotel.

'But I believe you're interested in ghosts,' said Peter Chapman, the managing director. 'In that case, you might like to sleep in the Fiddler's Room. Nobody knows who he is or why he plays the violin for some guests and not for others. Quite a few swear they've heard him, even those who have not actually been sleeping in the room.'

No fiddler played that night but the legend is so deeply rooted that there must be something in it. Is it the last echo of Monmouth's riotous night?'

My appeal in West Country newspapers for information about haunted inns brought some ghostly skeletons out of hiding. What Mrs Alice Bushey of Truro told me of her experiences at The Castle in 1961 makes me wonder if there is more than one ghost walking these carpeted corridors, This is her story:

'I was travelling from London to Truro by road with my daughter. We broke our journey and stayed overnight at The Castle hotel at Taunton. After dinner and a chat in the lounge, we were shown into a bedroom with two single beds and, knowing we had to start off early next morning, we soon went to sleep.

'I cannot tell you how long I had slept, but I was awakened by a quiet rustling sound as if someone was sighing; thinking it to be my daughter dreaming I dozed off to sleep. Again I was disturbed by a soft movement around the foot of my bed. It sounded as if a hand was gently smoothing the bedclothes, so stealthily that had I not previously heard the sigh, I might have taken no notice, but it continued for quite some minutes. I became wide awake and, thinking my daughter was wandering around, I spoke to her and asked her why she was out of bed. The fact of doing that awakened her, she called and asked me why was I walking around the bedroom Funnily enough, we both had had the same experience and, not feeling too happy, slept from then on in the same bed!

'While we were having our breakfast I described the incident to some guests who were at the next table and to my dismay and horror one of the guests said, "Oh, didn't you know that you slept in Bloody Judge Jeffreys' room? That room is haunted!"

'I had never before believed in ghosts but I can assure you my opinion changed on the spot. And, it was so real that neither of us would go upstairs to get our luggage.'

The Lady with the Lamp

116 ELEPHANT AND CASTLE, Yeovil.

A Bass Charrington house in Middle Street in the town centre. Open: 10.30 to 2.30 & 6 to 10.30. Sunday: 12 to 2 & 7 to 10.30. Serves food as well as drink. Accommodation. Parking. Nearest station: Yeovil Junction, or Yeovil (Pen Mill). Telephone: Yeovil 3184.

THE LADY with a lamp who haunts the top floor of this pub disdains the use of doors. She makes her exits through a locked wardrobe.

This is how a GPO worker, staying at the inn, described the ghost to Trevor Kavanagh, a reporter of the *Bristol Evening Post*: 'She was about 24 and was wearing a long white gown and headdress, I could not see her hair. She held what looked like a sword hilt with a glowing light on the top.'

He said he was awakened at about 5 o'clock in the morning to see the figure of a woman standing over the bed of a friend who was sharing the room. 'It was the light that woke me. I was terrified and put my head under the sheets. She was only there for about 4 or 5 seconds before she disappeared through the wardrobe.' His companion slept through the incident undisturbed.

The description of the lady with the lamp tallies with that given by another visitor who had seen the ghost about six months earlier and with the description given by Mrs Christine Sword, the landlady (1970), who has been a spiritualist for 25 years.

'It is the figure of a woman, petite in a long gown and wearing some sort of head covering,' said Mrs Sword. 'She carries a lamp, or maybe it's a candle. We presume she was a maid on the premises at one time, since she makes a lot of noise with what sounds like crockery and cutlery. But I am quite satisfied she is a happy soul.'

Staffordshire

The Figure in the Attic

117 ROYAL OAK INN, Abbots Bromley.
An Ansell's/Allied Breweries house 4½ miles north-east of Rugeley on B5234. Open: 10.30 to 3 & 6.30 to 10. Sunday: 12 to 2 & 7 to 10.30. Nearest station: Rugeley (4½ mls.). Telephone: Abbots Bromley 327.

ONE WINTER NIGHT in 1955 a guest at this inn removed by mistake a wooden peg which fastened the door to the attic. Drawing aside the curtain across the inside of the door he saw 'the white figure of a man with a bushy beard.' The guest did not stop to chat and when he and others returned minutes later to search, the attic room was bare. Some weeks afterwards the landlady encountered the ghost when she woke in the night. 'I saw a figure of a man going into the bathroom,' she said. 'He seemed to have on a long cloak-like garment. I was petrified and dived under the clothes.' But the haunting does not stop there. A strange musical sound emerges at odd times of the day and night from a fireplace in the bar. It is similar to the music from an old musical box, although it has never played for long enough to allow a tune to be recognised.

The Woman in White

118 THE GREYHOUND AND PUNCHBOWL, Bilston.
A Butler (of Wolverhampton) house in the High Street. Open: 10.30 to 2.30 & 6 to 10.30. Sunday: 12 to 2 & 7 to 10.30. Lunches. Nearest station: Bilston (via Birmingham). Telephone: Bilston 41660.

A FASCINATING pub with carved panelling and plaster-worked ceilings and the ghost of a woman in white seen to sweep down the stairs of this one-time Stow Heath Manor House. It was built during the Wars of the Roses on the old 'cruck' principle using giant tree trunks—one for each of the four gable ends and one for support in the centre—as a framework around which the house was shaped.

The Arm of Glory

119 WHITE HART INN, Caldmore Green, Walsall.
*An Ansell's house on the outskirts of Walsall. Open: 11 to 2.30 &
6 to 10.30. Sunday: 12 to 2 & 7 to 10.30. Sandwiches. Nearest
station: Walsall. Telephone: Walsall 33458.*

IN A GLASS case in Walsall's library museum there is a mummified
arm which was found half buried beneath years of dust in an attic room
of the White Hart. Locally it was known as The Arm of Glory* and the
Victorians concocted all sorts of legends about it and the strange
protective powers it was thought to have.

But the medical school of Birmingham University upset all those
stories when they examined the arm and revealed it to be that of a
child, skilfully dissected by a surgeon for no more sinister purpose
than to use as a specimen in the school.

What the medics did not find an answer for was the origin of the
ghost that haunts the cobwebbed gloom up there beneath the rough-
hewn rafters of this building which was built as a manor house in 1560,
soon after Elizabeth had made herself comfortable on the throne.

History had moved on some 300 years when the ghost first walked.
The old manor had become an inn, the White Hart, and in some dingy
attic room a distraught servant girl had committed suicide by pressing
her tear-stained face to a hissing gas bracket.

From that day on there had been stories of hauntings, reports of
unexplained noises in the loft, of a mysterious handprint in the dust,
of a ghostly shape by the bed, of an intensely cold atmosphere.

One former licensee, an ex-RAF policeman, says: 'I wouldn't spend
a night in that loft for a £1,000. One Sunday I was sitting in the living
quarters of the inn—that's the floor below the loft—making up the
books. Then I heard the noises. It was like someone slowly pacing the
floor of the loft . . . *bump, bump.* I looked towards the door, which was
slightly open. There was one of the inn's dogs, a big Alsatian, standing
stiff, its fur bristling, looking up the stairs. That was enough for me.
I ran down the stairs as fast as my legs would carry me. Nothing would
persuade me to go up to the loft again.'

The wife of another licensee tells this story of the handprint in the
dust:

---

* Cyril T. Oxby, in his book *Believe it or Not* describes a Hand of Glory in these
words: 'A grisly talisman, a charm made use of by robbers. It was composed
of a hand, hacked from a gibbetted criminal, pickled in brine and the fat of the
dead man. A candle placed in the hand was believed to shed a light which
gave thieves immunity from arrest and caused others to fall into a deep sleep.'
The Victorians had it summed up in this little poem:

> Oh Hand of Glory, shed thy lite,
> Direct us to our spoil tonite,
> Flash out thy lite, oh skeleton hand,
> And guide the feet of our trusty band.

'My husband came across it in the thick dust on the table. It was a small print, something like a woman's hand and it looked as though someone had gripped the edge of the table. He asked me if I had been up in the loft but I hadn't, and no one else had been up there either. We still can't explain it to this day.'

Yet another licensee's wife adds weight to the coincidence:

'For no reason at all I woke up early one morning and saw something white standing at the foot of the bed, I did not wait to take a second look and dived under the clothes. It may have been a trick of the moonlight . . . I don't know. There was something strange about the White Hart Inn that was hard to explain. I always had the impression that someone was watching me.

'We did not make a habit of talking about it, in case we should frighten the children, but my eldest daughter also experienced the same sensation. I also heard the bumps from the attic. It was usually about three o'clock in the morning.'

Turn Again . . .

120 WHITTINGTON INN, Kinver.

A free house, non-residential on the A449 Wolverhampton to Kidderminster road, 3½ miles west of Stourbridge. Open : 10 to 2.30 & 6 to 10.30. Sunday : 12 to 2 & 7 to 10.30. Ample parking. Serves food. Nearest station : Stourbridge. Telephone : Kinver 2988 & 2496.

DICK WHITTINGTON wasn't quite the romantic rags-to-riches character the panto producers would have us believe. He was the youngest son of a man who was outlawed for marrying without the King's consent, but that didn't make him a penniless vagrant whose only friend was his cat. His father was Sir William Whittington of Kinver, Lord of the Manor until 1352 when he sold it for a pretty penny to Thomas de la Lowe.

Baron Fitzwarren, the shrewd London merchant to whom Dick was apprenticed, was a near neighbour and a close friend of Dick's old grandfather—on his mother's side. He agreed to take the lad into his service almost from the day Dick was born.

That said, it is safe to argue that young Richard Whittington didn't walk the highroad to London with all his worldly goods tied up in a red spotted handkerchief; it is more than likely that he made the journey from Gloucestershire riding comfortably on the back of a well-fed horse, with one of his father's servants riding beside him, as a bodyguard.

There is no doubt that he went on to become Lord Mayor of London, not once but four times, after the incident on Highgate Hill when he threw his hat in the air at the reassuring sound of Bow Bells.

Though he did very well for himself and made enough money to rebuild London landmarks such as Newgate, St Bartholomew's Hospital and the Gray's Inn Library he never attempted to buy back the old

The Whittington Inn, Kinver (No. 120)

family mansion at Kinver. That eventually became a pub, though not before Lady Jane Grey had spent part of her childhood there and left behind her a ghost that haunts a corridor on the first floor.

There is another haunting by a less aristocratic ghost, a monk who walks by day, seen once to pass through the solid oak door in one of the bars. Which is not surprising in a house riddled with hidden rooms, concealed staircases and secret tunnels, a reminder that life in Tudor England wasn't all a game of Kiss-me-Kate in the orangery.

There is a concealed staircase leading to a secret room in the attic, which used to be one of two Jesuit chapels. It is here that members of the inn's staff claim to have seen the ghostly monk. Said one: 'There was a time when I was working in the attic doing some electric wiring. I was surrounded by candles which kept going out. Yet you could put a candle here when a gale was blowing and nothing would happen to it.'

Mr Alfred Hogg was resident director of the Whittington Inn for 27 years but never encountered anything extraordinary. 'I believe there is something though,' he says. 'There is an atmosphere. In any case, it seems to be a friendly one.'

Another Ghost

But evidence of another ghost at the Whittington came to me by way of BBC disc-jockey Tony Brandon, on whose late night show I appeared one Christmas to talk about ghostly encounters. Listeners had been invited to write in telling of their experiences in haunted houses. It was Mr George Clarke of Sparkhill, Birmingham, who came up with this fascinating story:

'I had just left the army after serving seven years. I had worked in the officers' mess, so I was looking for a similar job in civvy street. I found this job at the Whittington Hotel as lounge waiter.

'I took over my small room which was one of three along a very narrow corridor. The first two nights were uneventful. On the third night or early morning I was awakened by a heavy weight or pressure on my feet and legs as though something was leaning over the bed and, at the same time, the pressure was around my throat. I was trying to shout out but could not. This seemed to last for an age and was very vivid. When my faculties came back I seemed to be fixed on my back hardly able to move. I lay like this till daybreak.

'When I saw the landlord I told him what had happened. I could see he did not disbelieve me. He said to me, "I suppose you won't sleep in the room again?" I said I would sleep there again on one condition ... During the four days I had been at the inn I had made friends with his bull mastiff dog; I suggested I take the dog into the room with me that night. The landlord agreed.

'I got into bed and the dog lay on the foot of the bed. I felt quite safe— until I was awakened again, but this time by the dog. He gave a growl and his head was moving from side to side as though he was trying to get away from something which was holding him. I got up and tried to pacify him but he was experiencing something devilish. The dog was certainly feeling the influence of something sinister in the room. We got out of it early. I could see the dog would not settle again.

'When the landlord came down to breakfast I told him what had happened. He then related what had happened before. A young lad had slept in the room and saw the apparition and struck out at it, banging his knuckles on the wall. A woman before him had the same sinister feelings as I had. After telling me this he took me up into the roof and pointed out a small altar which was directly over the room concerned.'

The Gentle Governess

121 SEIGHFORD HALL HOTEL, Seighford, near Stafford.
A Thwaites hotel, just four minutes from the M6 motorway. Normal licensing hours with 11 o'clock closing during summer months and all Saturdays. One hour supper extension. Accommodation: 13 bedrooms with private bath, and 'phone. Ample parking. Nearest station: Stafford. Telephone: Seighford 341, 342 & 394.

QUEEN ELIZABETH not only slept here; it was she who had this half-timbered mansion built and then made a present of it to Richard Elde, her Paymaster General to the Forces in Ulster.

Though she was a frequent visitor to Seighford during her 45 years on the throne, it is not her ghost that haunts the place. Neither is it a vengeful ghost of any one of the five Cavaliers whom Cromwell ordered to be shot when they were discovered in hiding in the inner hall. They left only blood stains on the floor.

It is in fact a gentle ghost, recognised in print by the hotel's owners, Thwaites of Blackburn. They give it this brief mention in their brochure: 'Seighford even had a friendly ghost, a governess who returned whenever a new governess was appointed. Note to the nervous—she walks no more!'

That may or may not be; but who was this ghostly governess? The present manager elaborates: 'This is not at all a bad-tempered ghost,' he remarked, though he pointed out he hadn't long been at the hotel and had not seen anything himself. All the same, he gave these details: 'It is the ghost of a young lady, who about 200 years ago was governess to the Elde household. She was deeply in love with the master of the house and when this was discovered committed suicide. Her ghost is said to search the house for the children under her care. If any young persons stay the night in Room 8 (which is apparently where this unfortunate business happened) she is supposed to appear and soothe their brows and then disappear.'

Next to Room 8 there is a part of the house to which no entrance can be traced. It is a space between two floors at the end of the building, to which there appears to be ventilation by two parallel slits in the beams. It is thought they may be air ventilations to a well-concealed priest hole, though there is one visible halfway up the back stairs.

There is someone who remembers the ghostly governess and the commotion her appearances caused. She is an old lady* of 85, the last member of the Elde family to live at Seighford Hall. This is what she remembers:

'A room on the third floor at the back of the house was approached by its own stairs which had a small gate at the bottom. This was the governess's room. Three governesses, who had never met, told the same story about their first night in that room.

'They heard the gate open and someone coming up the stairs. The door was pushed slowly ajar, making a noise over the rather rough carpet, and then they were aware of a dark figure bending over them and withdrawing silently . . . There was never any question of someone going up to the room and being mistaken for the ghost. No one seems to know how it came about or, if there was a ghost, the reason for the visitation.'

'The family always felt that it must have been a previous governess coming back to see if her successor was suitable to look after the children of the family.

'The second ghost was heard, but never seen, on the landing of the main staircase, outside the nursery . . . Three knocks would come on the door at midnight, followed by the rustle as of a heavy silk dress sweeping over the floor. The nurses would get up and throw open the door but nothing was ever seen.'

* Aunt of the present Richard Elde and mother of Major J. F. Huxford of Maplehurst, Sussex.

K.O. for a Ghost

122 NOAH'S ARK INN, Tipton.
A Wolves and Dudley house in Owen Street. Open: 11 to 2.30 & 6 to 10.30. Sunday: 12 to 2 & 7 to 10.30. Nearest station: Tipton. No telephone.

TOM CARTWRIGHT was a welter weight boxer with 600 professional fights to his credit. When he retired from the ring to become licensee of the Noah's Ark he knew how to look after himself in an argument with any other man. But tackling a ghost was quite a different matter.

The night Tom woke up and saw a figure at the foot of the bed about to strike him, he wasn't sure whether to duck or take a swing at it. He hit out and the figure disappeared, leaving Tom pawing the air.

A few nights later Tom's wife saw the same ghost and described it as 'a young man in his late teens, dressed in a heather mixture tweed suit. He had fair hair and brown eyes,' said Mrs Cartwright, 'and he certainly did not look like a ghost. He had the happiest, most contented look I've ever seen. When he saw me staring at him he just vanished.'

In the bar, customers identified the ghost as a previous landlord's 19-year-old son who had died suddenly years before.

A Ghost Afraid of the Dark?

123 THE PARK, Tipton.
A Mitchells & Butlers house in Park Lane East. Open: 11 to 2.30 & 6 to 10.30. Sunday: 12 to 2 & 7 to 10.30. Snacks and lunch. Limited accommodation. Parking. Nearest station: Tipton. Telephone: 021/557/3308.

LADY MAY was the seven-year-old daughter of a Leicestershire squire. When her father had business to do in Tipton he took his little daughter with him and put up at this inn, where Lady May had a room of her own in the attic. To someone so young it was always an exciting adventure, especially as she was often able to accompany her father when he went riding.

After one of these excursions Lady May had a bad nose bleed and on her father's instructions went to her bedroom to lie down while he went out again on a matter of some urgency. But the bleeding became worse and developed into a severe haemorrhage. Frightened by the sight of so much blood, the child tried to get out of her room to go for help, but the attic door had jammed. She was a prisoner and on the point of collapse. By the time her father returned that evening, and went to her bedroom to see her, little Lady May was dead.

Today dogs refuse to go near the attic and workmen, knowing nothing of the tragic story, have refused to work in it, because of the atmosphere they sense. They reported that something they were not able to define had touched them, an experience supported by the wife of a former landlord, Mrs D Harrison.

'I had a horrible experience up there,' said Mrs Harrison. 'I never liked that room, but we used to store our Christmas decorations up there. Well, one day I was sorting the decorations over, and—it makes me go cold to think of it—something brushed past me. I just knew something was near me. Then the door clicked shut very gently.'

The landlord who took over The Park after the Harrisons, heard footsteps upstairs and unexplained knockings and bangings. His Alsatian dog would not enter the attic room and many times people told him, 'Your upstairs lights are on, you know.' He would go up to the attic, turn off the lights, only to be told a little while later that they were on again. The switches are not faulty, nor could vibrations account for the phenomenon. Could it be that little Lady May was afraid of the dark?

The Manor
House, West
Bromwich
(No. 124)

The Little Old Lady and the Black-Bearded Man

124 THE MANOR HOUSE, Stone Cross, West Bromwich.
An Ansells' house, known locally as 'The Old Hall' in Hall Green Road. Open : 12 to 2.30 & 6 to 10.30. Two lounge bars and restaurant. No accommodation. Ample parking. Nearest station : Wednesbury. Telephone : 021/588/2035.

AT THE WAR'S end The Manor House was nothing more than a dilapidated muddle of buildings, hardly fit for its ghosts to live in. Despite a history going back to 1290, it looked at one time as if this priceless example of a medieval timber-framed building would fall victim to the bulldozer. But the skills of a perceptive architect and a team of dedicated craftsmen (backed by £24,500) saved it—ghosts and all.

Since it was taken over by Ansells' brewery in 1961 a number of people working there have seen or heard ghosts. They recount stories of unexplained voices singing and talking, of footsteps on the stairs, of the figure of a man with a black beard, and the outline of a little grey-haired old lady peering through windows.

The manager, Mr John Dryden, a practical, down-to-earth midlander, who did not believe the rumours he heard before opening The Manor, is now convinced the place is haunted. 'I have been forced to change my mind,' he says. So has his wife, his headwaiter and his secretary. The chefs are convinced and the cleaners, too.

Footsteps Upstairs

'The first incident occurred before the place opened to the public,' says Mr Dryden: 'I was alone in the building locking up when I heard footsteps in an upstairs room. I thought someone had been locked in accidentally and went up to see who it was. There was nobody there.'

Mr Dryden said his most frightening experience happened one evening around midnight when he was standing in the restaurant with his wife. 'There were just the two of us talking quietly when suddenly the door at the end of the restaurant opened and the air went cold. The plants at the bottom of the stairs rustled as if someone had walked past and then we heard footsteps on the stairs. It was uncanny. We could hear the steps and yet we could see nothing. On other occasions after that—always late at night—I saw the images of a man with a black beard and a little old woman with grey hair peering through the windows. At first I thought I was the only one who had noticed these things. Then the foreman electrician told me that he had heard voices singing and talking on nights when he was working alone in the building . . .'

Cleaners working at The Manor House in the early morning have had similar experiences. One, while cleaning upstairs, heard the sound of organ music and started to sing to it, believing it was coming from a radio downstairs, which later she found had not been switched on.

Another cleaner, resting in the downstairs bar after finishing her work for the morning saw something move across the room—'It was very dark and I thought it was the barman,' she says. 'I did not take much notice of whatever it was, and then, to my horror, it passed through the fireplace!'

On one occasion when a barmaid was checking stock with her back to the bar she heard a cough and a movement behind her, as if someone was at the counter wanting attention. When she turned to serve there was nothing but the empty bar. The chef in the steak bar has encountered the same ghost. 'I was in the kitchen when I heard a woman's voice in the dry cellar. I went to have a look, but could find nobody so I came up pretty smartly,' he said.

Mr Dryden recalls that his relief manager, while outside one evening getting a breath of fresh air, saw the image of an old woman, silhouetted in a window. He moved around thinking that what he had seen was nothing more than a trick of the light, but the figure remained.

This resulted in a West Bromwich girl spending several nights at The Manor House, watching for the little old lady at the window, who she believed to be her 80-year-old grandmother, who fifty years before had been burnt to death when she fell into an open fire in an upstairs room.

Investigating the hauntings at The Manor House brought to light a ghost at Ansells' Aston Cross Brewery, in the middle of industrial Birmingham.

'I only see the ghost when I am alone and working late,' says Mrs Joan Whitehead, cook at the senior staff dining-room. 'He always appears at about 5.15 pm and is dressed in a riding jacket, a stock and gaiters.'

The dining-rooms and kitchen at the Brewery are on the site of the old stables; it is therefore thought by some that the appearance may be the ghost of Mr George Hastilow who drove an Ansells' bottle wagon, always immaculately dressed in breeches, gaiters, brown boots and cravat.

The Crinolined Spectre

125 ST JOHN'S VAULTS, Wolverhampton.
A free house in George Street in the town centre. Open: 10.30 to 2.30 & 6 to 10.30. Sunday: 12 to 2 & 7 to 10.30. Nearest station: Wolverhampton. Telephone: Wolverhampton 20755.

LOCALLY this pub is known as The Flea and Fidget. Years ago when it was a boarding-house a middle-aged woman leapt to her death from the top floor. A former manageress claimed to have seen the ghost 'dressed in a blue crinoline.' The present manageress, Mrs Iris Pearce, has heard the sound of footsteps as if someone were walking on uncarpeted stairs.

'On occasions, for some unaccountable reason, my dog begins growling and will not go up to the top floor,' she says.

Suffolk

The Ghost in an Overcoat

126 THE CROWN, Bildeston, near Ipswich.
An Ind Coope house on the Stowmarket to Sudbury road (B1115). Open: 10.30 to 2 & 5 to 10. (Friday & Saturday to 11). Sunday: 12 to 2 & 7 to 10.30. Snacks at the bar. Accommodation: 5 bedrooms. Ample parking. Nearest station: Ipswich. Eastern Counties bus No. 283 passes the door. Telephone: Bildeston 510.

THIS IS a real chocolate-box pub; black oak beams, white painted plaster, a crooked upper storey under a higgledy-piggledy roof of moss-covered tiles, leaded lights looking out on to a cobbled path—every tourist's dream of ye olde English inn, and haunted into the bargain. It's genuine 15th-century—built as a wool merchant's residence in 1495 when Bildeston, along with most of west Suffolk, was having it rich from the weaving boom.

One wonders if the ghost—a man wearing an overcoat and an old-fashioned hat, seen standing in the private quarters of the house—stems from those early days. He could be the cause of the unaccountable footsteps heard at various times in different parts of this rambling building. But how about the loud hammerings at the front door, so loud that one landlord, suspecting rampaging louts, dashed upstairs and looked from a bedroom window directly above—and saw nobody, though the hammering went on. Could that be something to do with that wild day in 1855, when every window in The Crown was shattered, along with many a pint pot and drinking goblet. The Riot Act was read to the vast, excited crowd who, despite seven determined constables, had forced its way into the pub and set about drinking it dry.

The occasion was a Parliamentary election held under an extended franchise. The Crown, it seems, was the headquarters of one of the candidates. Perhaps the overcoated gentleman in the old-fashioned hat?

Ghosts by the Dozen

127 YE OLDE THREE TUNS, Bungay

A Prime catering house in the market place run in conjunction with King's Head Hotel. Open: 10 to 2.30 & 6 to 10.30. Sunday: 12 to 2 & 7 to 10.30. Food and accommodation at King's Head. Parking. Nearest station: Beccles (5 mls.). Telephone: Bungay 2117 or 2377.

CANON JOHN PEARCE-HIGGINS* and Mr Donald Page, a well-known medium, led an investigation into the hauntings at Ye Olde Three Tuns in the summer of 1969. After their enquiry they said there was evidence of about two dozen 'earth-bound entities' in the hotel.

One of the ghosts was thought to be of an 18-year-old youth named Rex Bacon, who hanged himself in the Three Tuns in 1682 after killing his wife's lover. Another was said to be Tom Hardy, an 18th-century highwayman who made the inn his base and returned to haunt the place after he had been hanged for his nefarious deeds.

* See footnote on page 133.

Surrey

The Heavyweight

128 THE GEORGE, Chertsey.
A Courage house in Guildford Street. Open: 10.30 to 2.30 & 6 to 10.30. (Friday and Saturday to 11.) Sunday: 12 to 2 & 7 to 10.30. Snacks and lunches Monday to Friday. No accommodation. Parking. Nearest station: Chertsey. Telephone: Chertsey 62128.

BEFORE Mr Edward Silver moved into this pub in 1960 he was told about the ghost by the previous licensee, who had heard furniture being moved around the bar at night, after closing time. But Mr Silver never took it seriously until he received a letter from a Somerset couple who had stayed the night. They told him about the strange happenings in their bedroom in the early hours of the morning.

'The atmosphere went tense and very cold,' said Mrs Eilean Creasly, 'and the next thing that happened was that someone sat on the foot of the bed. The bed seemed to go down in the middle with the weight.'

Mr Silver confirmed that although he had never seen any ghost, he and his wife had definitely heard unaccountable noises during the night.

'The creaks and groans never really bothered us,' he said. 'In fact I still don't know whether I believe in ghosts.'

The Locked Cupboard

129 MARQUIS OF GRANBY, Esher.
A Watney house on the A3 London to Portsmouth road. Open: 10.30 to 2.30 & 6 to 10. Sunday: 12 to 2 & 7 to 10. Serves morning coffee from 10.30. Lunch between 12.30 to 2. Parking for 200 cars. Nearest station: Esher. Telephone: Emberbrook 1031.

THIS IS a Dickens pub. He wrote of it in *Pickwick Papers* as the place where Sam Weller called on his mother and found her dispensing hot buttered toast and pineapple rum to the red-nosed Mr Stiggins.

Since Dickens never mentioned the ghost one must presume it was not haunting the pub when he knew it. Just how well acquainted he was with the Marquis can be judged from his colourful description of the place: 'The Marquis of Granby in Mrs Weller's time was quite a model of a roadside public-house of the better class—just large enough to be convenient, and small enough to be snug. On the opposite side of the road was a large signboard on a high post, representing the head and shoulders of a gentleman with an apoplectic countenance, in a red coat with deep blue facings, and a touch of the same blue over his three-cornered hat, for a sky. Over that again were a pair of flags; beneath the last button of his coat were a couple of cannon; and the whole formed an expressive and undoubted likeness of the Marquis of Granby of glorious memory.

'The bar window displayed a choice collection of geranium plants, and a well-dusted row of spirit phials. The open shutters bore a variety of golden inscriptions, eulogistic of good beds and neat wines; and the choice group of countrymen and hostlers lounging about the stable-door and horse-trough, afforded presumptive proof of the excellent quality of the ale and spirits which were sold within.'

What a different scene it is today and how vastly changed from four hundred years ago—the oldest part dates back that far—when it was a cluster of mud and wattle cottages huddled by a cart track.

And the ghost? The landlord and his family, who have been there for twenty years, claim there is one upstairs. They have heard her moving about, her skirts rustling and swishing as she walks. But that is not all. There is a locked cupboard that no one dares to open. In fact, to make sure that its secret is kept undisturbed, an enormous family Bible rests against the door.

The Night Coach

130 THE HOP BAG, Downing Street, Farnham.
A Watney house. Open : 10.30 to 2.30 & 6 to 10.30. Sunday : 12 to 2 & 7 to 10. Snacks. Parking. Nearest station : Farnham. Telephone : Farnham 02513/3270.

THE ONLY PUB that matters to the average tourist visiting Farnham is The Jolly Farmer, where William Cobbett was born on March 9, 1766. But a near neighbour in Downing Street is The Hop Bag, once known as the Adam and Eve. In those days, before the spread of the railways, it was a coaching house and the stage used to come into the town over Long Bridge, sweep up Downing Street and roll to a stop in the inn yard to change horses and set down or pick up passengers.

There was one frosty moonlit night when the coach from Guildford pulled in and the driver climbed purposefully from his box. He made his way to where a girl was standing in the shadows and hoarsely whispered to her the grim news; the man she was waiting to meet had been shot dead when the stage was held up on the outskirts of Farnham.

It is said that the girl who waited that night has been seen many times since, still waiting. What's more there have been reports from guests sleeping at the back of the inn who have been awakened at night by the hollow clatter of hooves and the crunch of wheels in the yard outside, a yard, which, when they have looked from their windows has been silent and empty except for the shadowy shapes caused by the bright moonlight.

There was another pub in Farnham, The Lion and Lamb, which is today a cafe and has a share in the ghostly girl of The Hop Bag. Some customers, sipping nothing stronger than their morning coffee, have seen her through the window—'a woman in fancy dress' is how they described her—standing by the pump in the courtyard. And it's not the only haunting at The Lion and Lamb. A former manageress recalls that members of her staff tried to sell cakes and, on another occasion, serve a meal to the ghost of an old lady whom they mistook for a customer more than once.

When the Tsar Slept Here...

131 KING'S ARMS ROYAL HOTEL, Guy Lane, High Street, Godalming.
An Ind Coope house on the old Portsmouth road (A3100) in town centre. Open: 10.30 to 2.30 & 6.30 to 10.30. Sunday: 12 to 2.30 & 7 to 10. Serves food. Accommodation: 14 bedrooms. Covered parking. Nearest station: Godalming. Telephone: Godalming 21545.

TSAR PETER the Great of Russia passed this way in 1698 and his stay, though only for one night, will long be talked about. The food he and his cronies consumed was enough to sink the King's Navy, which is what they had journeyed to Portsmouth to look at. There were 21 of them in the Tsar's party at the King's Arms and between them they ate:

> *5 ribs of beef weighing 42 lbs.*
> *1 sheep weighing 56 lbs.*
> *Three quarters of a lamb.*
> *1 shoulder of boiled veal.*
> *1 loin of boiled veal.*
> *8 pullets, and 8 rabbits.*

They helped it down with 30 bottles of sack and a dozen of claret. That was dinner.

At breakfast they had only a snack:

> *Half a sheep.*
> *1 quarter of lamb.*
> *10 pullets.*
> *12 chickens.*
> *87 dozen eggs, and salad.*

They drank six quarts of mulled wine and three quarts of brandy.

Back in London they lodged at the house of John Evelyn, the 17th-century diarist, who described them in his journal as 'a right nasty lot.' Which only goes to prove you can go off people.

The legend tries hard to blame the haunting of the King's Arms on to the Tsar and his very merry men by suggesting that the ghost which manifests itself by kicking off a pair of heavy boots between one and 2 am is one of the Royal Russian party.

It's just as likely to be Nelson disposing of his buckled shoes or, for that matter, Henry VIII glad to give his feet a rest. Both slept there. Henry not only gave the place its name but dubbed it Royal as well.

A Face in the Mirror

132 THE ANGEL HOTEL, High Street, Guildford.
A three-star Trust House hotel in the town centre. Licensing hours: 10.30 to 2.30 & 5.30 to 10.30. Sunday: 12 to 2 & 7 to 10.30. Luncheon and dinner served in the Crypt Restaurant. Accommodation: 27 bedrooms, 13 with bath. Garage accommodation. Nearest station: Guildford. Telephone: Guildford 64555.

A GHOST in late 19th-century military uniform seen in the mirror of a wardrobe was sketched by a guest staying at this hotel at three o'clock one January morning in 1970. Three months earlier, a woman staying in the same room—the Prince Imperial of France room—contacted the hotel switchboard and reported the presence of something supernatural and asked to be moved to another room.

The haunted room is Room No. 1 on the first floor overlooking Guildford's High Street. It is a double room, with a beamed ceiling and containing a very large wardrobe with a centre mirror about 7 ft. high and 4 ft. wide. It was in this mirror that the ghost was seen and remained visible for about half an hour, during which time the guest who saw it, sketched the image using a blue biro pen and a red paper napkin.

Soon after he first noticed it, he called to his wife to look. She could not see anything for about five minutes, but it then became visible to her also—the waist-length figure of a middle-aged man in an old Polish army uniform of about the late 19th or early 20th century. The figure had dark hair and moustache and a very compelling expression in the eyes.

It was not until the next evening during dinner in the vaulted crypt restaurant of The Angel Hotel, that the manager first heard of the haunting of Room No. 1, when the guest called him and said: 'What I am about to tell you is no joke.' He then related his story. The assistant manager of the hotel said the guest was a hundred per cent convinced he had seen this ghost and was eager to testify that his story was absolutely true.

A drawing of the ghost at The Angel Hotel, Guildford (No. 132)

(A Surrey Advertiser *photograph)*

The previous experience of haunting in this room was when it was occupied by a woman guest in November 1969. The *Surrey Advertiser*, reporting on the incident, said that the telephone switchboard flashed from Room No. 1 extension at about 8 pm but when the receptionist answered there was no reply. She went up to the room and found the woman standing in the centre of the floor, 'petrified.'

That was the first time anything unusual had been reported from Room No. 1, although there had been stories a long time ago of supernatural happenings in the next-door room, Room 3.

The Angel is Guildford's oldest inn with a 13th-century vaulted crypt, thought to be the remains of a White Friary. In 1345 the friars erected a 'fyshe crosse' to mark the place where the town's fish market was held. The cross was surmounted by a carved angel from which the inn took its name.

But from where this rambling but comfortable coaching inn acquired its ghost in the mirror is a mystery.

The Once-Only Ghost

133 WHITE HART, Pirbright.
A Friary Meux house on the A321 Worplesdon to Frimley road. Open: 10.30 to 2.30 & 5.30 to 10.30. No accommodation. Food served. Parking. Nearest station: Brookwood. Telephone: Brookwood 3266.

NO ONE seems to know how long this old whitewashed building has stood facing Pirbright's village green, or when it first became a pub. As London's suburbia stretches deeper into the Surrey countryside, one wonders for how much longer it will retain its rural quaintness.

Major J B Slowly, the White Hart's landlord ('The only two things I have ever done in my life are fighting wars and drawing beer' he claims) has records going back to 1628, when the inn was a gamekeeper's lodge. There are villagers who say that it dates back even further, to 1380, when Pirbright was part of the Great Windsor Forest, in which the King went deer-hunting.

The day Richard II fell from his horse while chasing a white hart was a good one indeed for the common folk hereabouts. There being nowhere for the bruised royal posterior to rest in comfort, the King decided there was an urgent need for hunting lodges cum ale houses and ordered four more to be built in various parts of the forest. Somewhat confusingly they were all named the White Hart.

A likely story—but it doesn't account for the pub's ghost: 'a dark man, with a black hat and a black beard,' seen only once in one of the bedrooms, according to a 1963 report in the *Woking News and Mail.*

Perhaps its once-only appearance is explained by the fact that Major Slowly is not only an ex-Army man but a small arms expert, with friends

The White Hart, Pirbright (No. 133)

and customers who are among the world's top marksmen. At Bisley time, with the famous ranges barely three miles away, the place is full of them.

The Mischievous Monk

134 THE GRANTLEY ARMS, Wonersh.

A Friary Meux house a mile or two south of Guildford, just off the Guildford to Horsham road (A281). Open: 10.30 to 2.30 & 5.30 to 10.30. Sunday: 12 to 2 & 7 to 10.30. Lunch and dinner served in restaurant converted from old skittle alley. Snacks at bar. No accommodation. Own car park. Nearest station: Bramley. Telephone: Bramley 3351.

THIS IS ONE of the prettiest pubs in Surrey, in a winding street full of charming old houses and opposite a bus shelter which would surely be a first prize winner in any Best Bus Shelter competition.

The mischievous monk of The Grantley Arms is a ghostly hangover from the time when a monastic resthouse stood on this site, catering for the casual wayfarer with bread and ale and a night's straw.

Until exorcised by an Irish Catholic barmaid, this gay ghost in monk's habit used to appear regularly at Christmastime. One year, not long ago, he pulled down all the festive decorations in the bar.

Or could that have been the gambling Lord Grantley, showing himself to be a poor loser? He once owned this pub as part of his estate but lost it to one of his servants in a game of poker!

Sussex

Mystery at the Druid's Head

135 DRUID'S HEAD, Brighton Place, Brighton.
*A Watney-Tamplin house, in Brighton Place. Open: 10 to 2.30 &
6 to 10.30. Sunday: 12 to 2 & 7 to 10. Serves snacks. Parking on
meters until 6 pm. Nearest station: Brighton Central. Telephone:
Brighton 2549.*

AFTER A MORNING of lingering in The Lanes, buying antiques yo
cannot afford, this is the place to go to re-charge your batteries. It'
been in the thirst-quenching business more than 450 years and wa
one of the 100 Brighton pubs to get a licence to sell beer when the Bee
Act came into being in 1830.

One can safely assume that the fishermen of old Brighthelmston
(a sprinkling of smugglers among them) used the Druid's. So did th
men who were in the cartage trade. They congregated here with the
great wagons before starting the long haul to London. During th
Regency invasion it was a favourite with the dandies and their gels.

It is said that two tunnels, now blocked, lead from the cellars of th
Druid's Head; one to the old Fish Market on the seashore and the othe
to the Royal Pavilion. By this route the Prince Regent received hi
supplies of illicit liquor, we are told.

Somewhere from this colourful past a ghost lingers. Perhaps
young buck who reached for his swordstick too late? A smuggle
caught in the act? Or possibly the Prince Regent, unable to be rid c
a troubled conscience?

The man who has been landlord for 30 years is quite convinced th
Druid's Head is haunted. So are his three daughters. All have see
and heard their ghost (though of late it has not been so active), but it
identity and origin remains elusive.

* * *

In 1965 another of Brighton's pub ghosts made newspaper headline
This was Charlie, the ghost that is said to haunt The Bugle Inn, a lat
Victorian house in St Martins street. Reports told of lights flashir
on and off, of doors being locked and then unlocked, furniture bein
mysteriously shifted about, even the familiar bumps in the night.

The Phantom Landlady
and the Cripple Girl

36 THE REGENCY TAVERN, Regency Square, Brighton.
A Watney house in Regency Square. Open : 10 to 2.30 & 6 to 10.30.
Sunday 12 to 2 & 7 to 10.30. Snacks. Nearest station : Brighton Central.
Telephone : Brighton 0273/25652.

BRIGHTON in the 1870's was a bawdy, boisterous place, where the Victorian Cockney went for a breath of the sea. That was about the time Gladstone was unpacking his bags in Downing Street and, as if to mark the occasion, The Regency served its first pint—of milk.

It began business as a dairy at the corner of the square, with a coffee shop next door and a cobblers' adjoining. Now they are all part of the tavern, which so literally stands in the shadow of its towering neighbour, the Hotel Metropole, that one could say it is the Met's local.

When the cobbler was still in business, a little cripple girl, who lived in a room over the shop, thought she could smell gas and jumped to her death in a moment of panic. She left behind her a ghost and a treasured possession, a pair of almost unused wooden clogs, which were discovered only quite recently in the cellar. But she is not alone in her haunting. For years The Regency had a landlady who held the licence for longer than anybody can remember—so long in fact that, since she died, her ghost too has remained in the pub that was so much part of her life.

She was not only one of the best-known characters in Brighton, but her two sons, learning the business from their mother, went on to establish a chain of pubs along the Sussex coast which have since been absorbed by one of the big brewery takeovers.

In his 'Picturesque Pubs' feature in the *Brighton Argus* Mr R C Millar wrote this about the haunting of The Regency: 'How long her spirit had been roaming the Tavern is not known for sure. But one of the first positive sightings was made by the son of a previous landlord who, soon after his father had taken over the pub, remarked how quickly his dad had taken in residents.

'Needless to say he had seen the resident ghost in the form of an old lady on the first floor who was no bed and breakfast guest. 'Twas the host and ironically enough no dog or cat that ever entered The Regency could ever be persuaded to visit the first floor without bristling collar or arched back.

'It took a special session by a medium with spiritually attuned friends . . to lay to rest the psychic manifestations.'

*   *   *

Not far away in Hamilton road, Brighton, there is a Charrington pub named the Prestonville Arms and that too has a ghost, which haunts the cellar. In the night crates of bottles are moved from one stack to another—noiselessly. Nobody has seen this ghost at work but the results of its nocturnal labours are plain to see in the morning.

The Castle, Chichester (No. 137)

194

A. N. Other?

137 THE CASTLE, Chichester.
*A Friary Meux house in West Street. Open : 10.30 to 2.30 & 6 to 10.
Sunday : 12 to 2 & 7 to 10. Snacks at bar. Accommodation : 2 bedrooms. Nearest station : Chichester. Telephone : Chichester 3185.*

ON ONE SIDE of this pub is Chichester Cathedral, on the other a theological college. And in the attic is a ghost.

A landlord's young son was so aware that someone unseen had joined him in his attic playroom that he went to fetch his father, during which time the contents of his pencil box were scattered over the floor. On another occasion three students from the near-by college were more than a little intrigued by the psychic phenomenon they witnessed —a cricket bat dropped unaccountably into the centre of the saloon bar—when they called in for a beer.

Regulars say the pub is haunted by the shade of a Roman centurion thought to patrol the old city wall which ends a few yards from the inn. In the cellar one can still see traces of the smithy wherein this pub had its beginnings in the 12th century.

The Phantom Snuff-makers

138 RED LION INN, Hooe, near Battle.
*A Bass Charrington house on B2095 between Ninfield and Pevensey.
Open : 10 to 2.30 & 6 to 10.30. Sunday : 12 to 2 & 7 to 10.30. Snacks
at the bar. Ample parking. No accommodation. Nearest station :
Bexhill. Telephone : Ninfield 371.*

AT ONE TIME only a mile of tidal marshland separated the front door of the Red Lion at Hooe from the open sea. It was so close as to make this an inn ideal for smugglers to run their contraband ashore with the foreknowledge that they wouldn't have much interference from the Revenue men. A row of lime trees growing outside was the recognised sign that the landlord was on the side of the smuggler and could be relied on to keep his mouth shut in return for a well-stocked cellar. In the 18th century, smuggling friends were not active only in the cellar. Up in the attic they operated a tobacco mill with which they ground plugs of baccy into snuff.

The mill is still there and, judging by the noises that come from the attic and the heavy-booted footsteps that sometimes pace the entire length of the roof space, it seems that the phantom snuff-makers are still as active as ever at their illicit trade.

The Queen's Head, Icklesham (No. 139)

The Haunted Landlord

139 THE QUEEN'S HEAD, Parsonage Lane, Icklesham.
A Courage house, about 200 yards off the main road (A259) between Winchelsea and Hastings. Open: 10.30 to 2.30 & 6 to 10. Sunday: 12 to 2 & 7 to 10. No accommodation. Serves food. Parking. Nearest station: Winchelsea. Telephone: Icklesham 238.

'SOME PEOPLE go to bed and read a book. I hop into bed and see spirits, sometimes six at a time.'

That's Charles Crundwell talking from behind the bar of his pub, The Queen's Head in the East Sussex village of Icklesham. This is more than a haunted pub; it has a haunted landlord to go with it, because ghosts seem to follow Charles Crundwell around. They manifest themselves to him almost anywhere and at anytime. It has been that way since a day in 1929 when, as a youth of 19, he saw his first apparition, the smiling image of a young, white-smocked laboratory assistant pouring something from a small glass bottle. He thought then that he was going out of his mind until his doctor diagnosed that he was psychic.

When he gave up acting in 1953 he took over The Queen's Head—and moved in on 'George,' the ghost of an old man, with beard, sideburns and a moustache, whom he has seen on several occasions, sitting in a chair by the fire in front of the bar. This ghost, seen in shirt sleeves and a rough tweed waistcoat sporting a heavy gold watch chain, is thought to be a former landlord named Gutsell, who after his death in 1890 was laid out in a coffin on the bar counter and given a rousing send-off by the customers.

Solid Ghosts

Mr Crundwell describes George as being 'as solid as a living person,' which is how he sees all the ghosts that come his way.

'They are not white and ghostly when I see them,' he says: 'They are not transparent. They all appear to me as normal people of flesh and blood, with this difference—each one I see looks like a subject in one of those old-fashioned, sepia-coloured photographs, bathed in an aura of glowing, golden brown.

'I have seen scores of people that way—but they are not people I know. If they were, I could perhaps explain that it was my subconscious wish that they should appear. Sometimes they are Chinese or coloured people. Always the features are animated, and the image lasts about half a minute to a minute.'

The Old Salt in the Cellar

140 THE SHIP, Hove.
A Watney's house, just off the sea front. Open: 10 to 2.30 & 6 to 10.30. Sunday: 12 to 2 & 7 to 10.30. Snacks, lunches and dinner. Accommodation: 6 rooms. Nearest station: Hove. Telephone: Brighton 734936.

SOON AFTER this seaside tavern opened its doors in 1702, there is little doubt that it became a profitable hunting-ground for the press gangs searching for the sailors to serve in Queen Anne's ships—and for the smuggling fraternity bent on finding the ideal hiding-place for their illicit shipments. Either activity could have provided a dark deed to account for the ghost of a seafaring man who is said to haunt the old cellars.

The Phantom Feet

141 KING'S ARMS, Rotherfield.
A Whitbread house on B2100, the Crowborough to Wadhurst road. Open: 10 to 2.30 & 6 to 10.30. Sunday: 12 to 2 & 7 to 10.30. Lunch and dinner. Snacks at bar. Accommodation and ample parking. Nearest station: Crowborough. Telephone: Rotherfield 465.

THIS PUB was once a tithe barn and here a miller who found the daily grind too much hanged himself from the ancient rafters. Yet it is not the ghost of the unhappy miller that haunts this mellowed hostelry.

Maurice Tate, the former Sussex and England cricketer, was once the landlord and after the experiences he and his family had they changed their minds about the existence of ghosts.

There was, for instance, the night Mr Tate went upstairs to the 'special' bedroom to get some money. He was so positive he felt someone touch him, that, believing it to be one of the children who had come into the room unheard, he asked 'What do you want?' When he looked round there was nobody to be seen.

Late in June the ghost has been heard to run up the stairs and along the passage above the bar. Several have heard it. Once in that upstairs passage, a pair of phantom feet appeared. They were not the feet of a miller with flour dust on his buckled shoes, but the naked feet of a young girl.

The Midnight Duellists

142 THE MERMAID, Rye.

A three-star hotel in the old town centre. A free house. Open: 10.30 to 2.30 & 6 to 10.30 (Friday and Saturday to 11). Restaurant and grill room. Accommodation: 24 bedrooms, 10 with private bath. Own car park. Nearest station: Rye. Telephone: Rye 3065/6.

A PARTY of excited Frenchmen that came over on a day trip in 1377 heartlessly burned down the original 'Mearmeade' along with the rest of Rye. Rebuilding the town was thirsty work which ensured that a new inn went up quickly on the old site. That building still stands today, though over the years it has been added to. At the same time it has collected a rich history, especially at the start of the 18th century when Rye was the Clapham Junction of the smuggling business. As a result, The Mermaid has a worldwide reputation for being the most attractive of all the smugglers' pubs. In addition it has acquired a ghost or two along the way.

The Hawkhurst Gang, who in their heyday were top of the smuggling league table, used The Mermaid as a meeting place. They were an unscrupulous bunch of ruffians led by a man named George Gray, who, after making a large, dishonest fortune as a 'gentleman,' retired before the law was able to pin anything substantial on him. He and his gang downed their grog at The Mermaid while they hatched their plans, argued out their differences and made the big decisions which could get them a cut throat or a small fortune.

There is an eyewitness account of the gang meeting at The Mermaid at the height of their power and insolence, after having run a cargo of goods on the seashore 'seated at the windows of this house, carousing and smoking their pipes, with their loaded pistols lying on the tables before them, no magistrate daring to interfere with them.'

Hell To Pay

If they did interfere there was more than hell to pay, as on a February night in 1737 when the High Bailiff of Sussex put up at The Mermaid, planning next day to serve writs on various members of the gang. At the instigation of a smuggler named Thomas Moore, the Bailiff was set upon in his bedroom, dragged by his heels down the stairs and into the street.

As he was hauled feet-first over the cobbles, of what was then Middle Street, writs, bail-bonds and personal belongings were tossed contemptuously after him from a window of the inn. He was flung on to a ship in Rye Harbour, which in those days, before the sea had receded, was at the bottom of Middle Street. While the gang argued whether to slip moorings and take their prize across to France, they were interrupted by the crew of a revenue sloop.

That Bailiff was lucky to escape with his life. In 1736 an Admiralty report revealed that 'the number of officers who have been beaten, abused, and wounded since Christmas 1723, was no less than 250, besides six others who have actually been murdered in the execution of their duty.'

There is little doubt that the Hawkhurst Gang's nasty habit of roughing up the other customers was not good for business at The Mermaid. The Mayor and Corporation stopped using the place for official functions in 1751 and soon after the inn closed its doors.

Could a place like The Mermaid, with such a wealth of smuggling activity not possess a smuggling ghost? The legend-makers have tried hard. There is a brief mention by Leonard Thompson in his *Romantic Old Inns* of 'a fair maid of Rye who loved a smuggler bold; unfortunately the fair maid's ardour triumphed over her wisdom and so at midnight her ghost wanders fretfully among the labrynth of rooms.'

But when The Mermaid was reopened on the eve of World War II it had acquired a swashbuckling ghost to add to its timbered charms. It was not reopened as an inn but as a private hotel and club run by Mrs May Aldington, mother of the novelist Richard Aldington. During her time at The Mermaid a fascinating ghost story came to light. In her booklet describing the inn Mrs Barbara Pearce relates how Mrs Aldington 'discovered' this ghost.

'There had been rumours of a haunting in the Elizabethan Chamber on the night of October 29th and one year a lady, claiming to be "psychic" asked to sleep in the room on that night. Mrs Aldington joined her. The lady slept well, but during the night, Mrs Aldington awoke to find a duel raging around her. The combatants were dressed in doublet and hose, fighting with rapiers. The victor disposed of the body of his opponent by throwing it down the oubliette in a corner of the room, now alas blocked up.'

Along the passage from the haunted Elizabethan room, with its great four-poster bed, is a bedroom named after Dr Syn, the fictional

Inn sign of The Mermaid, Rye (No. 142)

smuggler made famous by Russel Thorndyke. It has no ghost, but cunningly concealed in the guise of well-stocked bookshelves at the side of the Caen-stone fireplace, is access to a well which was used as a hiding-place for contraband. It is also the entrance to a secret escape to the bar below, a bar which has a massive fireplace spread across the whole width of one wall.

Halfway up that black cavern of a chimney is a priest's hole—you can see it if you stand inside the fireplace and look up—which no doubt saved many an agile freebooter from being clapped in irons.

The Ghost with a Funny Face

143 THE WISHING TREE, Hollington, St Leonards.
A Whitbread-Fremlins pub. Open: 10 to 2.30 & 6 to 10.30 (Friday and Saturday to 11). Sunday: 12 to 2 & 7 to 10.30. Snacks at the bar. No accommodation. Parking. Nearest station: St Leonards. Telephone: Hastings 51473.

WITH A NAME like The Wishing Tree anything can happen. This pub has a ghost with a funny face which starts the dogs howling and small boys rolling about with laughter. What's more, it causes ladies to emerge hastily from the loo in a state of undress. By all accounts it's a friendly old thing. It is thought to be one of two elderly women who owned the place before it became a pub. It was they who planted the wishing tree in their garden many years ago.

Mr John Northwood who became landlord in 1968 says: 'I am convinced there's a ghost and it's of one of the old ladies. One night I was talking to a customer and heard, *bump, bump, bump* over my head. I thought that's Mike, our son, out of bed, and went upstairs. Yet he and his sister were still fast asleep. First it was the dog,' Mr Northwood recalls. 'She started howling for days on end for no apparent reason.'

More puzzling was his two-year-old son's side-splitting chuckles at all hours of the night. Usually he was a sound sleeper. 'It was obvious something was making him laugh, something which he called "Funny face", ' says the landlord.

John Northwood and his wife can remember the many times they sat in the kitchen of the pub and felt an unseen something brush past them. John's brother from London, without knowing about the ghost, remarked on the very first night of his stay that there was something 'odd' about his room.

The Northwoods are not the only ones to have encountered the ghost of the old lady with the funny face; the previous landlord and his family had similar experiences. And one must not forget the evidence of the couple who were driving past The Wishing Tree one morning in the early hours and just missed running down a woman in old-fashioned dress, pushing a pram across the road. She just wasn't there when they got out of their car to remonstrate with her.

The Crab and Lobster, Sidlesham (No. 144)

Sir Robert's Last Stand

144 CRAB AND LOBSTER, Sidlesham, near Chichester.
*An Ind Coope house. Open : 10 to 2.30 & 6 to 10.30. Lunch, dinner
(except Sundays) and snacks. Parking. Nearest station : Chichester.
Telephone : Sidlesham 233.*

FIFTY YEARS before Domesday records were compiled there was an
inn at Sidlesham. It was the local of the Saxon longboatmen, whose
ships lay at a wooden pier close to where today's Sunday sailors tie
their dinghies. The present pub, of flint and whitewashed brick, with
beams of oak dragged from the wreck of a Spanish galleon beached
at Bracklesham, was built in 1723. Prisoners from the Highland rebellion
helped to pull down the old tavern and put up the new.

The smuggling gangs who infested the Selsey Peninsula helped to
drink the beer. They were always good customers—despite the nearness of the Revenue men who had a look-out at Pagham Head—and
dropped in for a quick one by way of the twisting, half-hidden pack-
horse trail leading up from Bracklesham Bay.

Today this pub is the haunt of wildfowlers, who, with their assortment
of friendly and ever eager dogs, roam the saltings where there was once
the bustling harbour of Pagham, a harbour that served Nelson in his
time, and before him many a Royalist fleeing to France.

Call here on a winter evening, when the mists creep close like a
stalking cat; talk to the marshmen or the fishermen while you thaw out
in front of the spluttering logs and get them to tell you about the ghost
of Sir Robert Earnley. He was one of King Charles's men, defending
Chichester which was a Royalist stronghold, though much undermined
by the espionage activities of the city's fifth column. On the day of the
city's surrender to Cromwell's men, Sir Robert, with his two nephews
and an escort of two cavaliers, galloped south to Sidlesham to make
contact with the local boatmen who organised the Royalist escape
route to France. Word of their getaway was leaked to the Ironside
commander, who sent a force of his cavalry after them.

Hacked To Death

Outside the inn, within sight of the ship that was to get them out of
England, Sir Robert was attacked and mortally wounded. His two
nephews were hacked to death. The details of the ambush vary with
the telling of the tale. Some say that Squire Earnley died, sword in hand,
outside the Quay House, opposite the Crab and Lobster. Others add a
touch of colour and tell you he was carried to the inn gasping his last
breath, to die on the aleroom floor. On one thing they are all agreed :
between them those five Royalists—helped no doubt by the regulars
from the Crab and Lobster—killed fourteen of Cromwell's men, and left
behind them a ghost, a tall uniformed figure, a cloak about his shoulders,
seen usually in the small hours before dawn; seen too in the vicinity of
the quay where that tremendous fight took place.

Captain Peter Robinson, the man who runs the Crab and Lobster, talks matter-of-factly about disturbances in the night, of footsteps which cannot be explained and the eerieness of an attic room which his cat refuses to enter. He admits to leaving the room unoccupied and giving it a miss when he has to get up in the night to investigate strange noises.

It makes one wonder if the history books are wrong. Perhaps Sir Robert died in this attic room of the inn, hidden there by his Royalist supporters who had hoped to ship their wounded leader to the Continent?

Warwickshire

The Grief-maddened Lover

145 THE WHITE SWAN, Harborne, Birmingham.
*A Mitchells & Butlers house in town centre. Open : 11 to 2.30 & 6 to
10.30. Sunday : 12 to 2 & 7 to 10.30. Nearest station : Birmingham.
Telephone : 021/454/2359.*

THE PUB was locked up for the night, the bars had been tidied and
everything had been put away. Mrs Davis, the landlord's wife, was
resting after a busy evening. Suddenly the dogs scrambled to their
feet expectantly, as if someone was coming. Their hackles began to
rise and with their tails between their legs they ran from the room.
Mrs Davis went very cold. 'A cold wind blew through the room as if
all the doors and windows had been opened,' she said. Then she heard
footsteps but could not see anyone.

The White Swan, Harborne (No. 145)

Had she seen the ghost it would probably have been of John Wentworth, a man of property in old Harborne, who was secretly courting a poor local girl. They met daily in a back room of The White Swan.

To ensure she reached there safely he provided a coach, which one day overturned as it careered through the town. She was thrown out and died of her injuries in the back room of the inn, to which she had been carried. John Wentworth went mad with grief. He shot his dog, then shot himself.

The Moody Ghost

'He makes his presence felt in one particular room,' said Mrs Davis: 'We none of us like that room. He does no harm, really, but he can be a nuisance at times. He has his moods and can be awkward, taking things like cuff-links and trinkets, no matter how carefully they have been put away; they are found in the oddest of places. He has been known to tap people on the shoulder if they are moving about in his favourite part of the house.'

The Runaway Stagecoach

146 THE PHANTOM COACH, Canley Lane, Canley, near Coventry.
A Mitchell and Butler house on the old coach road to Birmingham. Open: 10 to 2.30 & 6 to 10.30. Sunday: 12 to 2 & 7 to 10.30. Lunches and dinner (from 8). Parking. No accommodation. Nearest station: Coventry. Telephone: Coventry 72540.

STRICTLY SPEAKING this is not a haunted inn, but an inn which takes its name from a haunting. Hereabouts the London-to-Birmingham stagecoach ran off the highway and turned over into a swamp one wild night having made a last change of horses in Coventry. It was not an uncommon accident in the pre-railway era of the 'flyers' and 'quicksilvers' of the road. Since then many late-night travellers, motorists among them, have reported seeing a phantom coach on the stretch of road nearest the inn and a ghostly coachman trying desperately to hold in check four frightened horses as the coach swayed and rolled silently towards them.

The Philandering Farmhand

147 THE BLUE LIAS, Stockton, near Rugby.
A Whitbread pub, a mile off the Southam to Dunchurch road
(B4100). Open : 10.30 to 2.30 & 6 to 10.30 (Friday and Saturday to 11).
Snacks at the bar. No accommodation. Ample parking. Nearest
station : Leamington Spa. Telephone : Southam 2249.

ON A HOT summer's day you can sit beside the still waters of the Warwick and Napton Canal which cools the footings of this pub and reflect on its curious name. Outside a placid looking brontosaurus, all of 130 million years old, swings from the signboard, obviously as perplexed as you are as to why he's there. Inside, the landlord's daughter, Miss Virginia Powell, has the answers.

'Lias,' she explains, 'is another name for clay or stone formed in horizontal layers. This clay was on the surface of Britain some 130 million years ago. The climate was humid and the land swampy. This was the time of the prehistoric monster. Bones of a prehistoric monster have been found in the clay around here.

'The Blue Lias inn is probably the only public house in the world with a prehistoric monster painted on its sign.'

The inn was originally an 18th-century farmhouse. It is haunted by the ghost of a red-haired farm labourer who was killed by an enraged farmer who returned from market one day to find his wife in bed with the red-head.

'My father saw this red-haired figure passing through the bar on one occasion,' says Virginia. 'He was about to say "Good morning" when it disappeared.'

Only between March and November is this ghost active, though there is one particular room upstairs which is always cold and has an eerie atmosphere about it. Footsteps for which there are no explanation are heard late at night and in the early hours of morning. Similarly, there is no normal explanation for the sudden ice-cold atmosphere that customers have experienced at the bar.

'It is a sudden draught that sweeps through and disappears as quickly as it comes,' says the daughter of the house.

Maybe because of its chilly approach, the ghost with red hair is not the only attraction at The Blue Lias. The landlord's collection of framed pictures of vintage cars and old aircraft guarantees a lively line in conversation.

Wiltshire

The Gliding Monk

148 THE KING AND QUEEN, Highworth.
*A Whitbread house in the town centre. Open : 10 to 2.30 & 6 to 10.30
(Friday and Saturday to 11). Sunday : 12 to 2 & 7 to 10.30. Snacks
at bar. Parking. Nearest station : Swindon. Telephone : Highworth
293.*

THE LANDLORD of The King and Queen claims to be the only licensee
insured against ghosts. He has a £100,000 policy against a ghost
turning nasty, giving customers heart attacks or causing their hair to
go grey. The ghost that most concerns him is the furtive figure of a
13th-century monk which haunts this 600-year-old pub—once a coaching inn and before that a courthouse in the ancient Wiltshire town of
Highworth.

Like so many landlords he didn't believe in ghosts until something
extraordinary happened to make him change his mind one night when
all his customers had gone home and he was alone in the pub,
clearing up.

Out in the cobblestoned innyard, where the coaches used to stop
on the road from Swindon to Burford, two Alsatian guard dogs started
howling. 'They were howling in a most peculiar way,' recalls the landlord: 'Quite unlike their normal barking. When I went out, instead of
rushing up to greet me, the dogs were crouched side by side—straight,
rigid, their tails sticking out, their hair bristling.

Up The Wall

'I looked in the same direction as the dogs and saw the figure of a
man like a monk move very swiftly across the far end of the yard, where
the stables used to be. It was a normal three-dimensional figure and it
glided—that's the only word you could use to describe it—up the wall
and disappeared.

'Only then did I realise this was something extraordinary. The dogs
were all right again immediately the figure disappeared, though they
did not sniff around the wall. I just wish now that I had taken more
notice. It wasn't frightening. In a way I wish I could see him again.'

Others who have seen the three-dimensional monk of Highworth

The Haunch of Venison, Salisbury (No. 149)

describe him differently: a disfigured hunchback, say some, no more than four-foot-six tall. Thirty years ago, when he was first seen, it was in the daytime and the man who encountered him was the verger at the church. Tunnels are said to lead out from the church under the Market Square connecting the crypt with the site of the former monastery, a few doors up from The King and Queen.

The Ghost that Wouldn't Go West

149 HAUNCH OF VENISON, Salisbury.

A Courage/Anchor house in Minster Street, within sight and sound of the market place. Open: 10 to 2.30 & 6 to 10.30. (Friday Saturday to 11.) Sunday: 12 to 2 & 7 to 10.30. Lunches and dinner. No accommodation. Street parking nearby. Nearest station: Salisbury (Fisherton Street). Telephone: Salisbury 22024.

TRADITION-LOVING Americans so envied this tavern that an exact reproduction—beams, panelling, carving, tilted floors, the lot—has been built in the United States. But their copy is minus the ghost. The original tavern claims a white lady seen from the rear windows which overlook the tiny graveyard belonging to the church of St Thomas, with which the inn was probably associated when it was built, of wattle and daub, in 1320, two centuries before it was first licensed. The sound of unexplained footsteps coming from the upstairs rooms between 11.30 and midnight is another piece of authentic atmosphere missing from the American version.

Worcestershire

The Erring Wife

150 BLACK HORSE, Kidderminster.
*A two-star Banks house in Mill Street in town centre. Open : 11 to 2
& 6 to 10.30. Sunday : 12 to 2 & 7 to 10.30. Lunches and dinner.
Accommodation : 20 bedrooms. Parking. Nearest station : Kidderminster. Telephone : Kidderminster 3958 & 2782.*

THE WIFE of its very first landlord is thought to haunt this pub, parts
of which date back to the 17th century. She was in love with a coachman
who drove into town twice a week. On those nights she would creep
from her husband's bed to where her lover waited.

On one such night her husband followed her and shot them both
as they embraced at the foot of the stairs.

Stealthy footsteps sounding along an upstairs corridor, across the
ballroom and down the stairs are thought to be made by the ghost of
the woman on her way to keep a spectral date with her coachman lover.
Several guests and successive landlords have heard them. One landlord, quite recently, took a loaded shotgun and searched in vain for
burglars.

The Screaming Babe

151 ROYAL OAK, Upton Snodsbury.
*An Allied Breweries house on A422 Worcester to Alcester road.
Open : 10 to 2 & 5.30 to 10.30. Sunday : 12 to 2 & 7 to 10.30. Food
(Steak Bar). Parking. Nearest station : Worcester (6 mls.). Tele-
phone : Upton Snodsbury 631.*

IN 1961 this pub was given a brewers' facelift. The work included the
conversion of some adjacent old cottages into an extension of the bar.
It was to one of these cottages that a father returned home late one
night in the 1750's and, enraged by the persistent crying of his baby
daughter, threw her from the bedroom window. The father was subsequently hanged for the murder of the child, who left behind a pro-
testing ghost heard once a month, crying at first and then giving a
surprised scream, which ends abruptly.

Yorkshire

Epitaph to a Ghost

152 THE FLEECE, Elland.
A Younger's house in Westgate. Open: 11.30 to 3 & 5.30 to 10.30.
Sunday: 12 to 2 & 7 to 10.30. Snacks at bar, lunches. Parking.
Nearest station: Huddersfield. Telephone: Elland 3129.

A WEATHERWORN tombstone in the graveyard of Elland Parish
Church bears this epitaph:

> Be warned ye thoughtless,
> Ne'er that place frequent,
> Where precious time in sinful pleasures spent,
> Where sinners meet and revel all the night,
> And mix in riot, drunkenness and fight.
> Frequent it not, nor its bad company know,
> For there lo' I received a fatal blow.

The place the epitaph describes is a pub of quiet elegance, The Fleece,
a building of blackened stone, known once as The Great House, and
built originally in 1590.

It acquired its ghost in the last 200 years since it became an inn,
which, possibly when the industrial revolution was still in its infancy,
and liquor flowed cheaply, was a place of 'drunkenness and fight.'

How otherwise did Leathery Coit, as he was known locally, come to
be murdered in a room upstairs, his body dragged across a bedroom
floor and down the stairs, leaving a trail of blood-stains as a permanent
reminder of the killing? No amount of scrubbing by landlords over the
years has been able to remove the dark brown patches on the wooden
steps or the print of a blood-covered hand on the panelled wall. Even
if they did, there remains the ghost of Leathery Coit.

There are regulars of The Fleece who still talk about this spectral
character. He was last seen years ago by a man and his wife, as they
returned home late on a January night. Wind gusted quite suddenly
along the street and then they saw the ghostly form of Leathery Coit
furiously driving his carriage and pair down Dog Lane towards Old
Earth, having come from the direction of the old stables adjoining The
Fleece.

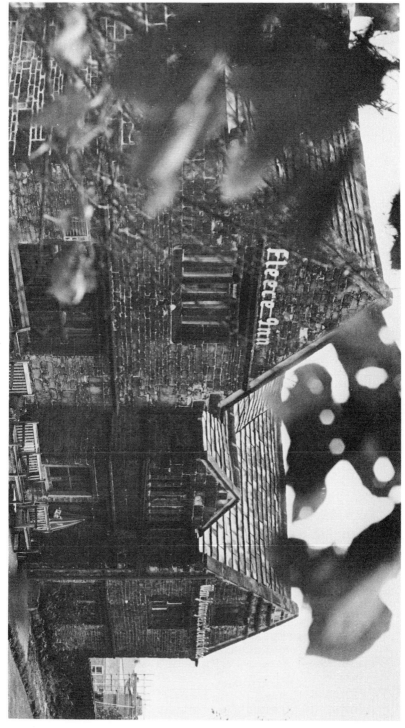

The Fleece, Elland (No. 152)

Iron Ned's Victim

153 THE BLUE BALL, Soyland, Ripponden, near Halifax.
A Whitbread house on the Rochdale-to-Ripponden road (A58). Open: 11 to 3 & 5.30 to midnight. Lunch and supper. Limited accommodation. Parking. Nearest station: Littleborough. Telephone: Ripponden 3232.

THE ROMANS were the first to build a pub here in AD 71. It stood at the side of the military highway and no doubt whetted many a Legionnaire's whistle on the long march from Chester to York.

If you go down into the cellars and look hard you can see the Roman masonry among the boulders brought down from Soyland Moor to make foundations for the inn when it was completely rebuilt on the original Roman site in 1672. Some time between then and 1846 when it was 'modernised,' The Blue Ball became notorious as the meeting place of coiners, highwaymen and gamblers. It also became haunted by the ghost of a serving girl named Faith, who was seduced and ultimately murdered—drowned on the moors—by a ruthless 18th-century landlord known as Iron Ned. 'It was described as suicide in the accounts of the day,' says Major Denis Siddall, the present landlord, 'but everyone secretly knew he'd killed her. On quiet winter nights you can hear her ghost run across the floor of Iron Ned's bedroom trying to escape his clutches.'

FAT NOTE: One of the most notable families associated with The Blue Ball was the Rudmans. Mrs Rudman, known as 'Fat Ann' weighed 19 stones and her husband tipped the scales at 21. No lean pair, but not by any means the heaviest on record. Edward Bright, who used to frequent the Black Bull of Maldon, Essex, and drink a gallon of small beer a day, weighed 44 stones when he died on November 10, 1750, aged 30. After his death, to settle a bet, seven men were buttoned inside his waistcoat 'without straining a button or breaking a stitch.'

The Whistler

154 THE SAXON HOTEL, Kiveton Park, near Sheffield.
A Samuel Smith house in Station Road, Kiveton. Open: 10.30 to 3 & 6 to 10.30. Sunday: 12 to 2 & 7 to 10.30. Snacks at bar. Parking. Nearest station: Kiveton. Telephone: Kiveton 770517.

THREE HEFTY flesh and blood policemen once sat in the cellar of The Saxon waiting for the ghost to walk. They waited among the barrels and crates for four hours without seeing so much as a mouse move. But successive landlords at The Saxon, which was newly built in 1960 at the cost of £40,000, have seen and heard sufficient to be convinced that the inn is haunted, but by whom or what is not a hundred per cent certain.

The Saxon Hotel, Kiveton Park (No. 154)

Some say the ghost is of a monk who was murdered long ago. He haunted houses in the vicinity of The Saxon for years before the inn was built. He was always known locally as Jasper and thought to be from a chantry which used to be on the site of the inn.

Jasper's mark of distinction is his whistle, the kind of whistle used for attracting someone's attention.

'The first time I heard it I thought someone was at the other end of the cellar,' said the original landlord of The Saxon, Mr Harry Blackburn. 'But I was alone. I heard the whistle again. Still no one was there but I felt an eerieness in the air as if someone was with me.'

Once Jasper's presence was so overpowering that the landlord had to leave his refrigerated cellar for the reassurance of the bar.

Since then the ghost has been heard with regularity, padding around the cellar. It rarely invades the landlord's living quarters, though occasionally its been heard in the concert room.

'I don't believe in ghosts, but you have to believe what you hear,' says Mr Les Fletcher of The Saxon. 'I was in the cellar when I heard the sound of a switch being touched and someone coming down the cellar steps, apparently wearing carpet slippers. Everyone else was in bed, and when I looked round there was no one there.'

When Fred Walks...

155 THE GROVE INN, Wakefield.
A Watney/Wilson house in Grove Road. Open: 11 to 3 & 6 to 11. Sunday: 12 to 2 & 7 to 10.30. Lunches and dinner. Parking. Nearest station: Wakefield (Westgate). Telephone: Wakefield 76817.

ANYTHING EXTRAORDINARY that happens at this pub is blamed on to Fred, the resident ghost. It first made its presence felt in 1959 when the daughter of the landlady, Mrs Stella Hudson, complained of a terrifying sensation of being smothered while in bed. The same thing happened when one of the three sons of the family occupied the bedroom. There have been other unusual incidents such as mirrors being smashed and heavy furniture being moved, suggestive of poltergeist activity.

The Grove Inn, Wakefield (No. 155)

Acknowledgments

TO ALL 'Mine Hosts,' particularly those who generously share their house with a ghost, may I say thank you gentlemen for your fascinating stories and for the assistance and co-operation I received from you in the preparation of this book.

Similarly a great many private individuals have helped me in one way or another. Some have given me information, or put me in touch with a friend of a friend. Others have loaned me books or sent me photographs. There are those who have supplied cuttings from long outdated magazines and others who have gone to great lengths to make notes from old documents and papers. To all I say a sincere thank you.

In particular I would like to acknowledge the help of Mrs Barnard of Bishops Stortford; Mr Phillip Bennett of Herne Bay, Kent; Mrs D. M. Bowles of Eastleigh, Hampshire; Mr W. Branch Johnson of Welwyn, Hertfordshire; Mr R. F. Brigden, Welwyn Garden City, Hertfordshire; Mr R. L. Brown of Basingstoke; Mr Peter Burgess of Balham, London, S.W.12; Mr Francis Bywater of the Faversham Society; Mrs Alice Bushy of Truro, Cornwall; Mr John Camp of Amersham, Buckinghamshire; Mr George Clarke of Sparkhill, Birmingham; Mrs L. M. Critchley of Bow, London, E.3; Mr E. Copeland of Henley-on-Thames; Mr Crossley of Woodford Wells, Essex; Mr L. H. Douch of County Museum, Truro, Cornwall; Mr Martin Das of London, S.E.7; Mr Laurence Dopson of Newdigate, Surrey; Mrs Alice Dobson of Stone, Staffordshire; Mr Richard Elde of Seighford, Staffordshire; Mr B. S. Elliott of Portslade, Sussex; Mr Andrew Green of Whyteleafe, Surrey; Miss Janet Gregory of Leicester; Mrs S. Gregory of Taunton, Somerset; Mr R. Helms of Charlton, London, S.E.7; Commander Peter Harper, R.N. (Rtd); Mrs L. R. Hellier of Ilfracombe, Devon; Major J. F. Huxford of Maplehurst, Sussex; Mr Edward King of Lymington, Hampshire; Miss M. McLachlan of Cheadle, Cheshire; Mr James Mann of Forres, Scotland; Mrs Mary Maslen of Nottingham; Mr Roger Newman of Liphook, Hampshire; Miss D. H. Pascall of Weymouth, Dorset; Mr W. H. Paynter, Curator of the Cornish Museum, East Looe; Mr Arthur Percival of the Faversham Society; Mr Stephen Price of Trull, Somerset; Mrs J. M. Rees of Deptford, London, S.E.8; Mr Alan Reeve-Jones of Herne Common, Kent; Mr Raymond Richards of Gawsworth Hall, Cheshire; Mr Norman Schofield of Weston-super-Mare, Somerset; Mr Les Smith of Mark & Moody Ltd., Stourbridge, Worcestershire; Mr Robert Songhurst of Maidstone, Kent; Mrs E. Steward of Winchester, Hampshire; Mr A.

Stratford of Chesham, Buckinghamshire; Mr R. B. Stucke of Shooters Hill, London, S.E.8; Mr D. B. Tubbs of Borough Green, Kent; the Rev. John Westlake of Weston-on-the-Green, Oxfordshire; Miss C. I. Whale of Riding Mill, Northumberland; Mrs M. K. Williams of Guildford, Surrey; Mr Gordon Wright of Nottingham; Mrs Janet Jarmany, Clayton-le-Dale, Lancashire; Mrs J. L. Everett, Gravesend, Kent; Mrs G. Guy, Nottingham; Mrs B. E. Olisa, Nottingham.

I am indebted to Messrs Hutchinson and Sons for permitting me to quote at length from Mr Fred Bason's writings in *The Saturday Book* (Nos. 9 and 10) edited by Mr Leonard Russell and to Messrs Frederick Muller for letting me quote from *In Search of Ghosts* by Mr James Wentworth Day. My thanks also to Mr R. C. Scott and Mr Christopher Barrett of West of England Newspapers for allowing me to quote from *Devon Tales of the Supernatural*, written by Mr Barrett for the *South Devon Journal*. Similarly I wish to say thank you to all those newspaper editors and their editorial and library staffs, who either gave me the freedom of their files in my search for haunted inns or sent me fistfulls of cuttings, from which I have liberally quoted. Several of the county, city and borough libraries came to my rescue over the more obscure details of local history, though there can be no denying that those who felt the full impact of my inquiries were the staff of the City of Westminster libraries, particularly Mr B. S. Davis of the Interlending Department.

I am grateful to Mr Peter Evans of the Brewers' Society and to the brewers both large and small for their interest and co-operation. To Mr John Fox of Whitbread and his colleague Mr George Trench I offer an extra word of gratitude for their encouragement to write the book in the first place, and their sustained enthusiasm during the time of writing it.

My very warmest thanks go to James Wentworth Day for his magnaminous introduction, to Chris Thornton for the photograph on the dust cover as well as most of those inside, to Doris Bryen for her unstinted research, to Harry Deverson for his advice and guidance and to Mr Alfred Mills for letting me delve freely into his dossier on ghosts and hauntings, a lifetime's collection.

Further reading

ABOUT GHOSTS
Ghosts I've Met by Hans Holzer (Jenkins).
The Lively Ghosts of Ireland by Hans Holzer (Wolfe).
Apparitions and Ghosts by Andrew Mackenzie (Barker).
A Casebook of Ghosts by Elliott O'Donnell (Foulsham).
Gazetteer of British Ghosts by Peter Underwood (Souvenir Press).
Haunted England by Christine Hole (Batsford).
The Stately Ghosts of England by Diana Norman (Muller).
Ghosts and Hauntings by Dennis Bardens (Zeus Press).
Unbidden Guests by William Oliver Stevens (Allen and Unwin).
Haunted Houses by Joseph Braddock (Batsford).
In Search of Ghosts by J. Wentworth Day (Muller).
Ghost Hunters Road Book by John Harries (Muller).
Gallery of Ghosts by James Reynolds (Creative Age).
Ghost Writer by Fred Archer (W. H. Allen).
Lord Halifax's Ghost Book (Fontana).
Shane Leslie's Ghost Book (Four Square).
Screaming Skulls and Other Ghosts by Elliott O'Donnell (Four Square).
The Realm of Ghosts by Eric Maple (Pan).
Haunted Houses by G. C. Harper (Chapman & Hall).
Ghost Hunter's Game Book by J. Wentworth Day (Muller).
Ghosts and Witches by J. Wentworth Day (Muller).
The Sixth Sense by Rosalind Heywood (Pan).
Real Ghosts, Restless Spirits and Haunted Minds by Brad Steiger (Tandem).
Elliott O'Donnell's Ghost Hunters (Foulsham).
Guide to Dorset Ghosts by Rodney Legg (Dorset Publishing Co.).
Haunted Britain by Elliott O'Donnell (Rider).

ABOUT PUBS
At the Sign of the Flagon by Gordon Wright (Frank Graham).
English Inns by Thomas Burke (Longmans).
Inns of Sport by J. Wentworth Day (Whitbread).
Old Cornish Inns by H. L. Douch (Bradford Barton).

Inns of Kent (Whitbread).

Guide to London Pubs by Martin Green and Tony White (Sphere).

Riverside Taverns & Inns by G. Elliott Godsave and A. C. Crouch (Constitutional Press).

Taverns of London by E. H. Popham (Cecil Palmer).

Famous Old Inns (A series published by Hamilton-Fisher).

A Book of Inns (A series published by St Catherine Press; now out of print).

Recommended Wayside Inns of England by Peter Stanley Williams (Herald Advisory Service).

Old Inns and Alehouses of Rye by G. S. Bagley (Rye Museum).

Scrapbook of Inns by Rowland Watson (Werner Laurie).

Old Inns of England by A. E. Richardson (Batsford).

English Inns and Roadhouses by George Long (Werner Laurie).

Surrey Pubs by Richard Keeble (Batsford).

London Pubs by Alan Reeve-Jones (Batsford).

Oxfordshire & Buckinghamshire Pubs by John Camp (Batsford).

Kent Pubs by D. B. Tubbs (Batsford).

Sussex Pubs by Rodney Walkerley (Batsford).

East Anglian Pubs by Vincent Jones (Batsford).

Old Inns and Taverns of Cornwall by Frank Graham (Graham).

Famous Smuggling Inns by Frank Graham (Graham).

More Smuggling Inns by Frank Graham (Graham).

Romantic Old Inns by Leonard Thompson (Ancient House Press Ipswich).

Some Inns and Ale Houses of Chichester by M. J. Cutten.

English Inn Signs by Jacob Larwood and John Camden Hotten (Chatto & Windus).

British Inn Signs by Eric Delderfield (David & Charles).

Inn Signia by Brian Hill (Whitbread).

Quaint Signs of Old Inns by G. J. Monson-Fitzjohn (Herbert Jenkins).

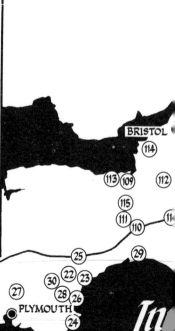

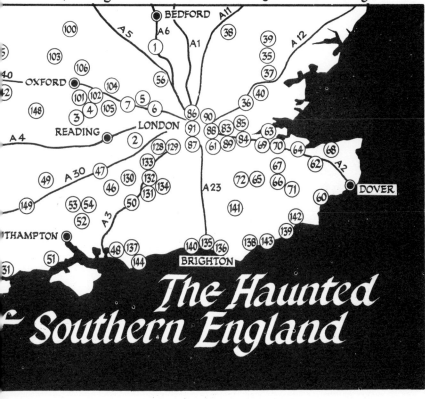

The Haunted Southern England